ALIKE AND DIFFERENT

Exploring Our Humanity With Young Children

REVISED EDITION

Bonnie Neugebauer, Editor

with a foreword by Carol Brunson Phillips

National Association for the Education of Young Children
Washington, DC

OCT 2

Photo credits: Cover (clockwise from topmost photo)—© Karen Phillips, © Gerald Lim, © Virginia Reed, © Nancy P. Alexander, © Cleo Freelance Photo; pp. v, 19, 43, and 159—© Bonnie Neugebauer; pp. 1 and 123—© Hildegard Adler; pp. 4, 38, 46, 109, and 112—© Nancy P. Alexander; pp. 7, 9, 14, 17, 34, 52, 55, 62, 65, 69, 76, 94, 106, 129, and 136—© Subjects & Predicates; p. 13—© Jeffrey High Image Productions; p. 21—© Gail Lynch; p. 28—© Vivienne della Grotta; p. 30—© Robert Samuel; p. 45—© Faith Bowlus; p. 51—© Quiel Begonia; p. 58 © Lori Thompson; p. 67—© Elaine M. Ward; pp. 73 and 132—© Michael Siluk; p. 80—© South Carolina Educational Television; p. 83—© Shia Photo; p. 87—© Loran Fogelman; p. 89—© Stephen Doxzen Photo; p. 91—© Toni H. Liebman; p. 96—© Barbara Rios; pp. 99 and 103—© Francis Wardle; p. 115—© Mary Harrison; p. 117—© Jim West; p. 141—© Marilyn Nolt; pp. 145, 147, and 149—© Bm Porter/Don Franklin; p. 153—© Jim Bradshaw; p. 156—© Renee Stockdale. *Illustration on p. 25:* © Lisa Mathias.

Originally published by Exchange Press, Inc., P.O. Box 2890, Redmond, Washington 98073.

National Association for the Education of Young Children
1509 16th Street, N.W.
Washington, DC 20036-1426

The National Association for the Education of Young Children (NAEYC) attempts through its publications program to provide a forum for discussion of major issues and ideas in our field. We hope to provoke thought and promote professional growth. The views expressed or implied are not necessarily those of the Association, and any mention of possible supply sources does not represent NAEYC's endorsement. NAEYC wishes to thank the editor and authors, who donated much time and effort to develop this book as a contribution to our profession.

Library of Congress Catalog Card Number: 92–061315

ISBN Catalog Number: 0–935989–52–8

NAEYC #240

Editor: Polly Greenberg; *Cover design:* Jack Zibulsky with Roxanne Everetts; *Book design and production:* Jack Zibulsky; *Copyediting:* Penny Atkins and Betty Nylund Barr; *Editorial assistance:* Julie Andrews

Printed in the United States of America

Contents

Foreword

Carol Brunson Phillips

The content of the education and socialization of young children is always a product of its time—changing as the context in which it occurs changes. For most children it becomes a special admixture of what the adults in their lives intend for them to learn both for now and for their future, along with what may unintentionally creep into their daily life experiences.

Right now we know that we are raising children to interact in a much different and larger social universe than our universe to-day—in a global economy and in a world community. Alongside this realization we also know that children must learn something different from what we have learned and that they are, right now, participating in both the intentional and the unintentional experiences that will shape their chances to have meaningful and productive lives.

Regardless of what we once may have thought, children do notice differences in people. Very early in life they learn that some differences make a difference and others don't matter, that some are most important and others less so. And as children attach meaning to those differences, they go about forming the intricate maze of knowledge and values, the development of which we still know so little about.

Yet we do know that in this world where children exist, negative values are attached to some human differences; and although we may underestimate the power of children to perceive the unspoken messages in their world, children will in fact come to learn them.

It has been said that actions, more often than not, speak louder than words. And if this is so in the case of childrearing, then we must be especially vigilant in our actions to shape the values that children will attach as they learn about the people in their world. If we don't they will learn by default the messages that are already prevalent out there in the world, and both we and they will contribute to perpetuating past ideas that we do not want to replicate for our children's future.

I have had the privilege of working for many years in a college of human development, preparing teachers and human service professionals for work with children and families. In doing so I, along with my colleagues, have discovered that true teaching and learning involves a powerful transformation process that creates new ideas from old ones and uncovers new relations in oneself and in the world. This process gives the power and responsibility to each of us to be deliberate in making value judgments about human worth.

CAROL BRUNSON PHILLIPS, an early childhood educator, has for 23 years been involved in writing, research, and teacher education, specializing in cultural influences on development. Currently she is executive director of the Council for Early Childhood Professional Recognition in Washington, D.C.

Chapter 1
BEGINNING

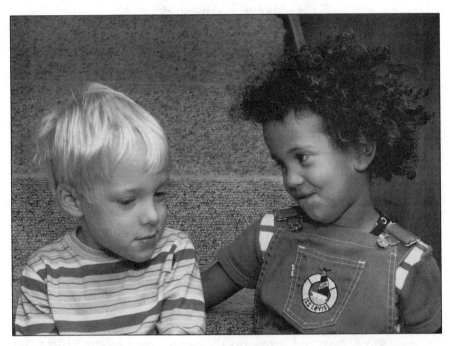

"All people, all children, have a common sameness that makes them part of the human race, the brotherhood of man. Sameness and difference should not be seen as opposites; they go together."

—*Francis Wardle*
Denver, Colorado

"It Isn't Fair!" Antibias Curriculum for Young Children

Louise Derman-Sparks

One morning in April, Jean arrives at the child care center clutching a stereotypic Indian warrior in her hand. Another child says to her, "Don't let Suzanne see that, Jean. It will hurt her feelings." (Suzanne, one of the staff, is Cherokee Cree.)

Donald, playing at home with his Lego® set, turns to his mom and declares, "You know, Mom, all of the Lego people in this set are White people. Why?"

Four- and five-year-olds at Pacific Oaks are beginning to identify, think critically, and care about the ways societal bias affects their daily lives. But why should young children be saddled with such issues, you may ask? Why do they need antibias curriculum?

We know that by age two, children begin to construct their gender and racial identity and their physical self-concept. We also know (Katz, 1982; Honig, 1983) that, again as early as two, the stereotypes, prejudices, and discriminatory practices pervasive in our society negatively influence this process. Our children grow up in a psychologically as well as physically polluted environment. Their developing attitudes toward themselves and others reflect the poisoning effects. They exhibit preprejudice—erroneous beliefs and fears that either mirror adult bias or that, although based on how young children think, may lead to prejudice unless adults intervene.

What are young children thinking and doing?

Steven is busy being a whale on the climbing structure in the two-year-olds' yard. Susie tries to join him. "Girls can't do that," he shouts. Steven may want to play by himself, or he may not want to play with Susie. Whatever the reason, he already has gender-based words for rejection in his repertoire.

Robby, three years old, refuses to hold a Black classmate's hand. He says "Yucky" when seeing pictures of African American children in books. At home, he insists, after bathing, that his black hair is now white because it is clean. His mother worriedly relates the incident to his teacher, wondering if he is already prejudiced. The teacher is also concerned. They plan activities to help Robby overcome feelings that can crystalize into full-blown prejudice.

Mark picks up a big block. "You're strong," Julie admiringly tells him. "You're strong, too," responds Mark. "No, I'm not," replies Julie. At the age of four, Julie never chooses large-motor activity, already confining herself to small-motor, quiet choices. Research tells us that by age four, children monitor each other's behavior.

"Ann can't play with us. She's a baby," Sandy tells the teacher. Ann, four-and-a-half years old, uses a wheelchair. Although walking is a signpost of movement from babyhood to childhood, it is also true that one major way in which handicappism is shown in our society is infantilizing disabled people. Thus, the preschool child's *understandable* comment is another example of preprejudice.

"You aren't an Indian," another four-year-old tells Suzanne. "Indians don't live anymore." We have found that preschool children already hold a number of erroneous and negative ideas about Native Americans. This may be the first bias young children learn in our society.

What is antibias curriculum about?

Antibias curriculum recognizes and provides tools for dealing with the issues raised by these anecdotes (which are only a few of the many we have collected). Grounded in traditional preschool goals and methodology, antibias curriculum enables children to comfortably explore the differences and similarities that make up our individual and group identities, and to develop skills for identifying and countering the hurtful impact of bias on themselves and their peers. Antibias curriculum goes beyond our earlier approach to curriculum at Pacific Oaks, which was focused on activities about people's similarities but did not directly address differences or *preprejudice*.

Pacific Oaks teachers state our goals as follows: "I want children to become tolerant, understanding, and compassionate by the time they are five." Molly Scudder, kindergarten teacher, asserts, "They need that as a base for the rest of their lives. We're providing emotional nutrition." Mae Varon, preschool teacher, adds, "I want children to learn to discriminate, to make judgments about what's fair and what's not, to sort out what they have the power to change

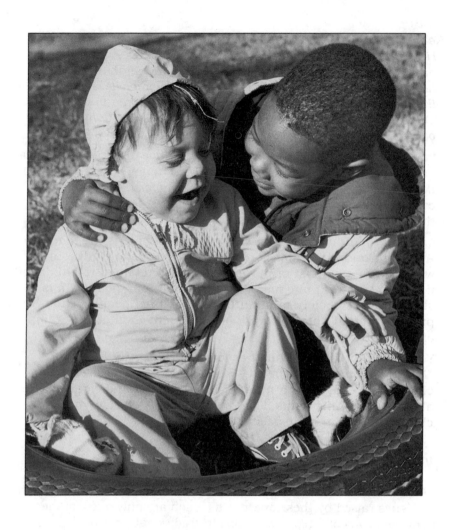

and what they can't do anything about." Maria Gutierrez, teacher of two-year-olds, continues, "We want children to become effective thinkers and problem solvers, not accepters of dogma—actors, rather than passive victims." "Children have the capacity for experiencing hurt and despair, and for empathy and fairness. What we are doing empowers them by increasing their understanding and teaching them ways of handling stress. That's more realistic than trying to protect them from knowledge of the world," concludes Cory Gann, preschool teacher.

Antibias curriculum is at once a methodology and a particular belief system that values diversity among people—and peaceful, just, and equitable cooperation. We found that it was not so much new methods that we needed, but rather thinking about activities from a new perspective and using existing methods for new issues.

What are the sources of the curriculum?

Daily curriculum emerges from three sources: (1) children's behavior, (2) teachers' awareness of children's developmental needs and learning styles, and (3) societal events. Sometimes the child's comment or behavior is the starting place: *A group of children are playing in the sandbox; the girls cook and the boys dig tunnels. One boy calls out to the girls, "We're finished working now. Get us our supper."* At group time their teacher decides to read one book about the different kinds of work women do and another book about men doing household work. The next day she helps each child make a book about what kinds of work, at home and out of the home, their own family members do, pointing out the diversity of roles.

Sometimes the teacher introduces an issue. Knowing that young children notice and express curiosity about skin color, the teacher of the threes plans a series of activities about this aspect of identity. She has them put their arms out in a circle and talk about each other's skin colors; look at themselves in a full-length mirror and talk about their own color; find the crayon and paint that most closely matches their skin, and draw a picture of themselves with it; and use beige, brown, and black as well as white drawing paper. She reads the book *Colors All Around Us* by Vivian Church (1971), which illustrates the different skin tones of African American children and is also a good starting place for other children; takes color photos of each child and staff member; and makes a poster of all the different skin colors in the classroom.

Sometimes an event in the child's larger community precipitates an activity; Thanksgiving is a case in point. In the weeks preceding this holiday, children are inundated with stereotypic images and messages about Native Americans. It is impossible to escape the television specials, greeting cards, store decorations, and children's books with one-sided versions of the Thanksgiving story.

Antibias curriculum challenges such bias and the already erroneous beliefs and fears that preschoolers have about Native Americans; thus, we suggest (1) introducing four- and five-year-olds to the real daily life of contemporary Native Americans through photographs, filmstrips, visitors, or accurate books; (2) critiquing stereotypic images in greeting cards, decorations, and books as unfair and untrue by comparing them to accurate images; (3) having discussions that allow children to talk about their fears and misconceptions (perhaps by using a story as a catalyst); and (4) not permitting the playing of *Cowboys and Indians*, explaining that such games are hurtful to real Native American children. (We might tell a story about one of our Native American doll's negative experiences with other children playing *Cowboys and Indians* as a catalyst for discussion.)

What are antibias activities?

Activities fall into three categories, which build on each other. Here are some that we have found useful:

• Exploring physical differences and similarities

Read *What Is a Girl? What Is a Boy?* by Stephanie Waxman (1976), which helps children understand that their gender identity is determined by their body parts—not by the clothes they wear, the things they like to do, or how they show emotions.

Activities for learning about skin color have already been described. Children also need help understanding (1) that skin color comes from their parents and (2) that there is a range of skin color within each family. Collect or take color photos of each child's family members. Make a book about everyone's family.

Young children are curious and sometimes fearful about disabilities. They need opportunities to interact with disabled children, to explore the tools disabled children use, and to learn about how to enable disabled children to be as independent as possible. Have crutches, a wheelchair, a hearing aid, and materials in Braille and sign language available for children to learn about and use. Purchase or make a few dolls with specific disabilities. Tell stories, for example, about the doll in a wheelchair going to her preschool the first day and not having any way to get up the stairs. Ask the children what could be done so that the child could get in and out of the classroom by herself.

• Exploring cultural differences and similarities

Gender roles. Preschool children's play choices are already strongly influenced by gender norms. Observe children's free play, and help them experience activities and materials they normally do not use. Sometimes environmental changes help (e.g., moving housekeeping equipment—stove, sink, etc.—to the block area encourages crossover and joint use). Sometimes more direct intervention is necessary (e.g., a *girl's day* each week in the block area until girls are comfortable using the blocks on their own). Modeling, visitors, books, pictures, and stories provide children with data about the many different behaviors displayed and jobs carried out by women and men. Consciously include roles that contradict prevailing stereotypes.

Ethnicity. This aspect of antibias education, under the name *multicultural curriculum,* exists in many early childhood programs. Unfortunately, the methodology often reinforces rather than challenges stereotyping. Activities tend to center on holiday celebrations, and on objects and food, taken out of context of people's daily lives. This is *tourist* curriculum. Children *visit* a culture for a day, or maybe for a little longer (if they are doing a unit), and then go *home* to a classroom that does not integrate different cultures into its own daily life. Moreover, by focusing on holidays we give children the impression that other people spend their time in ceremony instead of going to work, raising children—living.

Preschool children are developmentally ready to explore cultural differences in the context of each child's family's life. This means learning, for example, about how Sam's family, who are Japanese Americans, live their daily lives—who is in their family, what roles they play, what work they do, what objects they use in their daily life, what food they eat regularly, as well as what holidays they celebrate. Sam's classroom should include written signs and tapes in Japanese, artifacts used in his home in the dramatic play area, Asian dolls, books about Japanese American children, and authentic pictures and wall posters depicting the contemporary life of Japanese Americans in the United States.

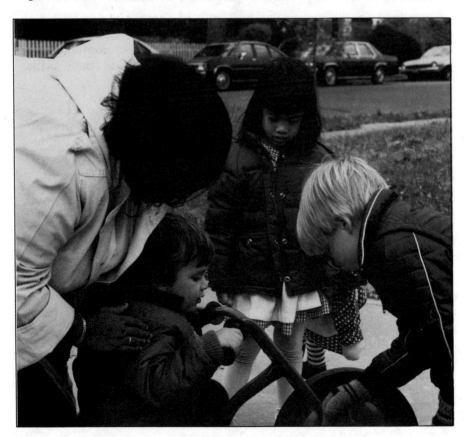

By basing ethnic cultural activities in the life of each child's family, we avoid the dangers of stereotyping a group by implying, for example, that *all* Japanese Americans live the same way. We avoid a *tourist* approach by placing cultural behaviors in context and by incorporating various aspects of each child's way of life into the classroom.

Find out from each family how they practice their ethnic heritage at home. Invite parents to school to tell stories about their family members and their history, to show objects, to cook foods, or to celebrate a holiday. Make books about each family's way of life; have a wall display of *Our Families*, with photos of extended family members doing a variety of jobs in and out of the home; and have books about different kinds of families. Learning about each child's family generates curriculum for a whole school year. If your class is ethnically homogeneous, begin with the differences among families in your class and then branch out, still keeping to the approach of individual families.

• Learning to challenge stereotyping and discriminatory behavior

Developing skills for challenging unfair behavior begins with one-on-one interactions between children. We already invest considerable time in helping them develop assertiveness and nonviolent conflict-resolution skills. Antibias curriculum extends these skills to discriminatory situations.

Role model nonacceptance of such behavior. Regardless of what you think may be the underlying reason, do not ever permit a child to reject another child because of gender, race, ethnicity, or disability, or to use derogatory terms about another child's identity. We consider such behavior equivalent to hitting or throwing a heavy object at another child, and we deal with it as we deal with physical aggression. We stop the behavior first, comfort the child who has been the target, and then find out from both what was going on and take action accordingly.

Develop critical thinking about stereotyping in books, television, and toys. Compare accurate photos and illustrations with inaccurate and stereotypic images. Explain how untrue pictures are unfair and hurtful because they make fun of people.

Involve children in group action. For example, Bill Sparks' mainstreamed, public school classroom faces the handicapped parking spaces. He noticed that a few teachers were not honoring the spaces. The children went to look at the parking spaces, then talked about the handicap sign and why these places are reserved.

Following a discussion of what to do, the children decided to make parking tickets to put on the cars of nondisabled teachers parked in the handicap zone. After a week of this activity, the spaces were left free for people who really needed them.

Another group action, this at Pacific Oaks, dealt with a frequently used object in children's lives. Lissa, a child care center teacher, decided one day to do something with the children about *flesh-colored* bandaids. She explained that the box said that the bandaids matched people's skin color; she suggested that they find out if this was true. Each child put a bandaid on and determined whether or not it matched his skin color. They made a chart of their results.

They then decided to have children from other classes also test the *flesh-colored* claim. Finally, they dictated and mailed a letter to the manufacturer. Eventually they received a letter with coupons for transparent bandaids! Although this activity was not sufficient to get the company to remove the *flesh-colored* claims from their boxes, it did teach the children about taking action when they think something is unfair.

How do you get started?

• Do some background reading (see "Within Your Reach—Resources on Diversity for Adults" on p. 175).

• Form a support group with whom to study, plan, and evaluate throughout the year. This group can include interested parents and teachers in your school or teachers from other schools. A support group empowers you to try new and possibly controversial activities and to make and learn from your mistakes.

• Begin with an aspect of antibias curriculum that you feel most comfortable with; judge what will work best in your setting.

• Plan how to involve parents (and administrators) from the beginning, informing and including them in developing activities.

We found that developing antibias curriculum is always stimulating, at times exhilarating, and at times painful. It has meant finding more effective means to put into practice our basic commitment to children.

The curriculum guide upon which this article is based is *Anti-Bias Curriculum: Tools for Empowering Young Children* by Louise Derman-Sparks and the A.B.C. Task Force, published by the National Association for the Education of Young Children, 1509 16th Street, N.W., Washington, DC 20036–1426; NAEYC order #242.

References

Church, V. (1971). *Colors all around us.* Chicago: Afro-American Publishing Co.
Honig, A. (1983). Sex role socialization in early childhood. *Young Children, 38*(6), 57–70.
Katz, P. (1982). Development of children's racial awareness and intergroup attitudes. In L. Katz (Ed.), *Current Topics in Early Childhood Education*(Vol. 4, pp. 17–54). Norwood, NJ: Ablex.
Waxman, S. (1976). *What Is a Girl? What Is a Boy?* Culver City, CA: Peace Press.

LOUISE DERMAN-SPARKS is the author of Anti-Bias Curriculum: Tools for Empowering Young Children, *published by NAEYC, and currently directs an antibias education leadership project funded by the A.K. Kellogg Foundation.*

Talking About Differences Children Notice

Elizabeth Crary

You and a group of preschoolers have just left the pet store. Carvis sees a tiny man and asks loudly, "Why is he so little? Did someone chop his legs off?"

Teresa and Gina are playing with blocks. Teresa's Aunt Alice comes to pick her up. When Alice bends over to help pick up the toys, Gina notices her withered hand and red skin from a birthmark. She asks in a curious voice, "Why is your hand so funny?"

Preschool children have a natural curiosity that helps them gather information about their world. In general, teachers and parents encourage this interest by responding promptly to their questions. However, there are times when children's questions embarrass adults who don't know how to respond. Questions about physical, ethnic, or racial differences are difficult questions for many people. When you respond abruptly or ignore the questions, most children conclude that something is wrong with them or with the other person.

Children also gather information by watching how adults respond to these people. If we are uncomfortable or ignore them, children often conclude that something is wrong with the person who is different. Here are 10 guidelines for dealing with awkward questions and for becoming more comfortable with different kinds of people.

• **Respond promptly.** If possible, answer the child's questions immediately. If this is not possible, tell the child when you will answer. Then, when the time comes, bring up the subject and answer the questions. Sometimes people are tempted to let the subject drift if the child forgets. That, however, gives children the message that the topic is too difficult or too uncomfortable to deal with.

• **Give simple answers.** According to Piaget, young children need simple answers that relate to their experiences and observations. "Why is that man so dark (or light)?" can be answered in terms of family rather than race. "He is dark because his mother or father is dark. You have blond hair and light skin just like your mother." Similarly, "Why is that man so little?" can be answered in terms of family rather than genetics. Preschool children have difficulty understanding abstract concepts—race and genetics are beyond their grasp.

• **Model respectful behavior both verbally and nonverbally.**
Smile and make brief eye contact as you would with any other pleasant stranger. Many people were taught as children not to stare. They were taught so well that they avoid looking at people with disabilities at all. One severely disabled man commented, "Sometimes I feel invisible. No one will look at me. I wonder what would happen if I fell down or fainted? Would people help me or step over me without seeing me?"

Respond to people with disabilities as you would to other people in the same group. Avoid acting as though they are mentally incompetent just because they are in wheelchairs. Let them answer their own questions rather than answering for them.

• **Respect a disabled person's body space.** Don't lean or hang onto a person or her wheelchair. Don't let children borrow crutches or walkers without getting permission first. In addition, resist the temptation to pat or touch disabled people in ways you would not touch others.

• **Acknowledge children's fears.** Some children are reluctant to approach or discuss people who are different from themselves. This often stems from a fear of the unknown or misconceptions about different people. Many children are suspicious of unusual people—like clowns or Santa Claus—as well as people with physical disabilities. These children resist the new and different. *Slow-to-warm* children need to be encouraged to gradually feel comfortable with unusual people.

Fears of disabled people are best treated as other fears: acknowledge them and offer children tools to deal with their fear. It is rarely effective to tell a child that there is nothing to be afraid of. If feeling comfortable were that simple, no child would be afraid. If you pressure a child, he has two problems—his fear and your disapproval. One helpful way to respond is to reflect the child's feelings—"You are scared of the man without legs"—and then give the child tools and experiences to deal with the fear.

• **Clarify misconceptions.** Children are often afraid of disabled people due to misconceptions. Many children think that bad things happen to you when you do bad things. (This idea is reinforced when children are punished for bad behavior.) In their eyes, someone with a visible disability must have been very bad. Another common misconception is that the deformity is contagious. The best way to respond is to clarify children's misconceptions.

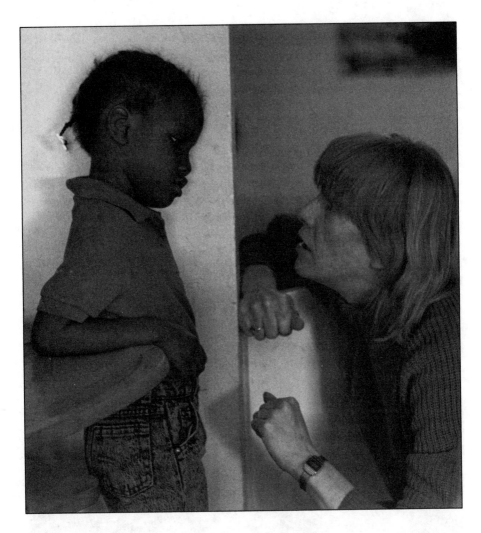

When a child has concerns, give correct information. "Simin has had cerebral palsy since she was a baby. She walks the way she does because it is the only way she can walk. It is not a sickness you can catch. The tiny part of her brain that tells her legs how to move does not work right. All the rest of Simin works fine and will continue to work fine."

In another case, a polio victim with a withered hand, you could say, "Mark had polio, a sickness, when he was a little boy. The sickness damaged the part of his brain that makes his hand work. He is well now. And nobody can get polio from him."

• **Offer help and let the disabled person decide how much help he or she needs.** Disabled people have a need to feel lovable and capable, as does everyone else. When people do things for them without asking, they receive a clear message that we think they are not capable of either doing something or deciding if they need help with it.

For example, if you are at the park and a woman in a wheelchair is having trouble opening the restroom door, you can ask, "Would you like some help?" If she accepts, you could ask two children to hold the door for her.

• **Model patience with people with disabilities.** Give people with disabilities the time they need to be independent. For example, when talking with a man who has a speech impediment, give him your undivided attention. Let him finish his sentence rather than finishing it for him. Your *assistance* carries the message that there is something wrong with the way he is talking (he is unclear or not fast enough). Don't pretend that you understand if you don't. It is often helpful to repeat what he said to clarify what you heard.

• **Introduce differences through books.** For some children it is less threatening to first learn about different people from a book. *Why Does That Man Have Such A Big Nose?* by Mary Beth Quinsey (1986) illustrates a variety of people (representing ethnic and physical differences) and answers common questions that children have in a simple, constructive way. *About Handicaps* by Sara Bonnet Stein (1974) helps children feel comfortable with people

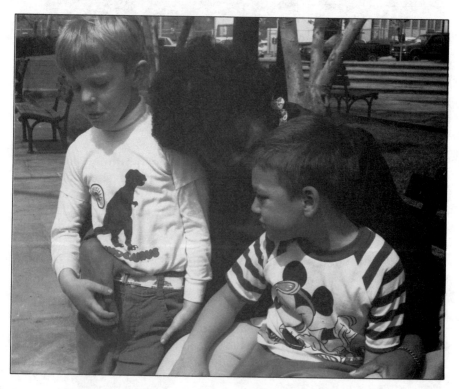

who have disabilities. *Why Am I Different?* by Norma Simons (1979) discusses differences in abilities and family styles.

• **Offer children experiences with real people.** When children have questions about a *different* person, consider letting them ask that person. Many people with disabilities welcome the chance to educate children. Look at the person. If he appears open and friendly, he may feel comfortable answering a child's questions. You may even know someone who would feel comfortable coming to your center.

Children live in a concrete world and are learning what is real and what is pretend. Children may want to touch a metal hand, ride in a wheelchair, or touch very wrinkled skin. If children can explore differences openly, they can begin to feel comfortable with all kinds of people.

Some children need to practice or replay what they have seen and learned. They may walk around blind, with crutches, or with uneven gaits. You can explain to these children, "It is okay to pretend to walk like a person with cerebral palsy in school or at home, but not when a person with cerebral palsy is around."

Children notice how the adults and children around them treat differences. It is important for adults to answer children's questions promptly, to verbalize unasked questions, and to model respectful behavior to all people. If adults are comfortable around people with disabilities, children learn that. If adults encourage children to talk about differences, children can clarify misconceptions and learn that differences are okay. When children have a chance to meet many kinds of people (people of different races and ethnic groups, people with disabilities), they can learn that friendship can accept both the commonness and the difference. You can offer children this gift of friendship by inviting different people to your center and by responding promptly to children's spontaneous questions.

References

Quinsey, M.B. (1986). *Why Does That Man Have Such A Big Nose?* Seattle: Parenting Press,.
Simons, N. (1979). *Why Am I Different?* Niles, IL: Albert Whitman.
Stein, S.B. (1974). *About Handicaps.* New York: Walker and Company.

ELIZABETH CRARY is a parent educator at North Seattle Community College. She is also the author of 15 books for parents, teachers, and children, and the president of Parenting Press, Inc.

"Where Do We Begin?" Bring the World Into Your Classroom

Bonnie Neugebauer

The richness and beauty of the world takes many forms—the craftsmanship of a basket, the feel and drape of a sari, the sounds of a lullaby. When we bring bits and pieces of the world into the daily life of our programs, the unfamiliar becomes familiar; what was outside our experience becomes part of our frame of reference. From that point on we have real objects and experiences that serve as a basis for asking questions and initiating conversations.

Classroom aesthetics

When selecting items with which to decorate your multicultural classroom, you may wish to consider the following: travel posters and magazine photographs that depict a wide variety of places and people (including people of different ages, abilities, and life situations); textiles from around the world on the walls and around the room in blankets, cushions, pillows, and rugs; drawings by children from other places and with varying ability; distinctive and interesting paintings, sculpture, pottery, baskets, and other arts; mobiles and wind chimes; printed labels in more than one language; a colorful hammock from Costa Rica; and containers for storage—pottery, baskets, calabashes, lacquered boxes.

Dramatic play

The richness of different cultures can be reflected in props for dramatic play—for example, teacups; chopsticks; baskets; gourds; kimonos; fans; getas; parkas; sarapes; African masks; mukluks;

saris; clogs; snowshoes; dashikis; moccasins; beads; berets; turbans; sashes; veils; fans; nets; futons; tatami mats; food containers, recipes, magazines and newspapers printed in other languages; foreign coins; variations of the playhouse (adobe, igloo, tent, mosque, oasis); dolls and puppets—Japanese daruma, Russian Matryoshka stacking dolls, and dolls with assorted racial characteristics and handicap equipment; stuffed animals, including camels, iguanas, goats, tigers, and snakes; and crutches, braces, heavy glasses, hearing aids, bifocals, and canes.

Music and movement

The wide variety of music from around the world can be introduced to children in the form of folk songs and recordings for children, translated and in foreign languages; classical, contemporary, and ethnic music recorded for adults, in English and in other languages; instruments from other places: Nigerian talking drums, thumb pianos, maracas, and bells (when possible, provide authentic instruments); and bossa nova, samba, jazz, and spirituals.

Science and mathematics

How about making science and mathematics as interesting as we know they are by using manipulatives featuring pictures of foreign objects; raw cotton; cocoa/coffee beans; chestnuts; lentils; feathers; seeds; plants (bonsai, orchid, cactus); foreign coins; sketches and photographs of skyscrapers, pyramids, and igloos in the block corner (from "Using Learning Centers for Multicultural Activities" by Elvia Ana Rodriguez and Kent Chrisman, *Texas Child Care Quarterly*, Fall 1985); and figures of varying ages, races, sexes, physical abilities, and occupations for block play.

Language

Try to find books that reflect a world view (see "Reflecting Diversity—Books to Read with Young Children" on p. 163), books in Braille, books in several languages, alphabet characters in other languages, and wordless books.

Taking up the slack

In all of this searching for interesting, available materials, there will undoubtedly be times when you can't find what you want. That's when you will need to tap your own creative resources and make your own materials.

• Write a book based on the lives and experiences of the children in your class. If you can't provide photographs, the children can draw the illustrations. Fill in with family photographs and magazine pictures.

• Find someone in your program who will make a doll to your specifications. There are many doll patterns available that will need to be modified only by fabric, color, and style choices.

• Let imagination fill in some spaces. Describe your vision to the children and let them adapt it to suit their needs.

• Write your own recipe book based on the favorites of the families in your program.

Chapter 2
MEETING THE NEEDS OF ALL CHILDREN

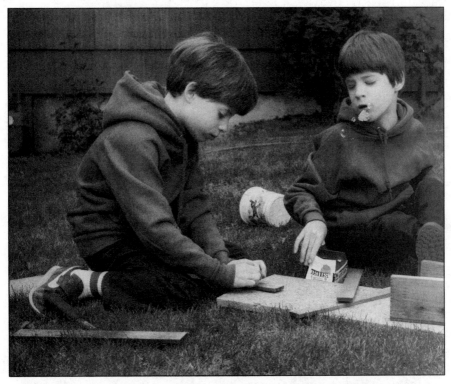

"Special needs are normal—everyone has them to varying degrees."

—Katie McGuinness
Adaptive Environments
Boston, Massachusetts

Obstacle Courses Are for Every Body

Carol Stock Kranowitz

Two children, as different from each other as chalk is from cheese, come to the same classroom every day at St. Columba's Nursery School in Washington, D.C. Nathan hurtles in like a cannonball, his treasure-laden backpack bouncing behind him. He is ready for the day, eager to join his friends, happy to converse and sing, nimble and quick in every way. He especially loves make-believe play, donning cowboy chaps or a king's cape and altering his tone of voice and facial expression to fit the role. He becomes the fearsome wolf, the biggest Billy Goat Gruff, or the mommy in the housekeeping corner with equal delight. Indeed, the only role he refuses to take in dramatic play is that of the baby or the littlest, proclaiming with vehemence, "I'm not a baby; I'm big!"

Nathan must protest frequently about his size because he is a person of short stature. (The preferred term for an individual like Nathan is short-statured rather than dwarf.) At the age of four, he is two-thirds as tall as his peers; he will never grow to a normal height. His legs are noticeably short in proportion to his body, causing him to lose his balance when he hops or stands on one foot. Otherwise, his compact body is well proportioned, and he enjoys more physical prowess than many of his classmates.

Ana is very different. A big little girl, she inches into school with extreme caution, just as she does into play, or conversation, or any new situation. Where Nathan leaps, Ana lingers; where he is outgoing, she is retiring; where he likes to be first, whatever the task or game, she prefers to watch and wait. Her shyness and physical development are normal and age appropriate for a four-year-old, yet they impede her initial participation in many preschool activities. Once in the game, however, she is in it whole-heartedly.

Both children have needs, but Nathan's short stature defines him as a child with special needs. As such, he is one among the 10% of children with special needs who are mainstreamed at St. Columba's Nursery School. Like the other boys and girls with differing disabilities, Nathan needs to feel good about his strengths and accomplishments, and to learn problem-solving skills in order to compensate for his difference. He needs to be comfortable with himself and with others who may treat him unfairly, and to mature as a well-equipped, social individual. Indeed, his basic needs are no different from Ana's or from any other preschooler's. All children have needs.

How, then, can a preschool meet the different needs of all of its children? The challenge is to find activities that do all things:

• specifically help those children who need a boost in any of the developmental areas—cognitive, physical, social, lingual, or emotional

• build on children's strengths and skills

• sit smack-dab in the mainstream of preschool life, so that they are shared experiences, not private therapy

• appeal to all children

• remain open ended in order to explore, not ignore, children's differences

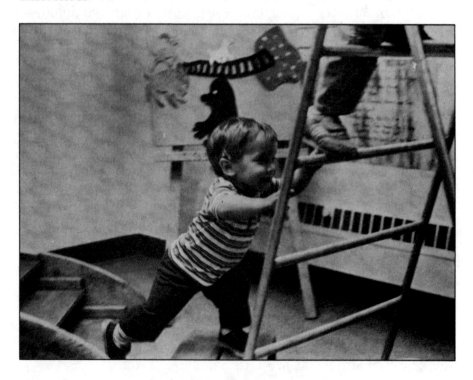

Creating meaningful activities for differing needs

Arriving at these ideal activities takes some creative thinking. **Begin positively** with a list of the children's strengths. Helping children to build upon the skills they already have, one small step at a time, is the surest way to achieve a greater goal.

Proceed to **determine the children's primary needs**. Ana's greatest need, for example, is to emerge confidently from her shell. Nathan's is to continue developing his many skills while learning how to function as a short-statured person in a world designed for larger people.

Set realistic goals. For instance, realistic goals are that Ana will feel comfortable about joining in the fun and that Nathan will have many opportunities to prove himself as a capable four-year-old. Unrealistic goals would be hoping for Ana to become the class leader or for Nathan to adore being mistaken for a toddler.

Next, **brainstorm** with your co-teachers about what **group activities** may be attractive to children with polar needs. All children like to draw to music, allowing the beat of the music to guide their crayons. Creative art work, such as making collages, is appealing. Choosing a song and leading the rhythm band works nicely. Class projects like cooking or planting a garden do not require special skills. For Ana and Nathan, an obstacle course is a perfect activity, as it encourages them both to develop their large-motor skills.

Select an activity, taking into consideration your own abilities and interests. It's easier to provide the children with a meaningful experience if the chosen activity is one that you enjoy personally. If you aren't keen on an activity, the children may not relish it either.

Plan and implement the selected activity with regard to the space and equipment available.

After you have presented the activity, **evaluate** how it went. Was it successful? Did the children stick with it? Was it too easy? Too hard?

Refine the activity. Try it again and again until you have a basic formula. When the exercise is worthwhile, the children will always let you know.

If you decide to proceed with an obstacle course, the success of the activity is guaranteed. Every child's body is different, but all bodies share the same need to climb, balance, and stretch. A child with superior athletic skills will enjoy an obstacle course because moving is his specialty. A sedentary child will like it, as she learns to maneuver her body in ways she never considered possible—or even desirable. A child with special needs will love it because it is a challenge he can meet in his unique style. In fact, preschoolers with special needs are so adept at making accommodations for their differences that they can teach their peers new ways of overcoming obstacles.

In theory and in practice, an obstacle course is a foolproof activity. Now all that remains is a little planning.

Problem-Solving Process

(the example used for Nathan and Ana)

1. Ascertain child's strengths

Nathan—imaginative, agile, healthy, outgoing, blessed with positive self-image

Ana—persevering, patient, compliant, methodical, aglow with each small success

2. Ascertain child's needs

Nathan—to prove that he is as competent as, or more competent than, his peers, despite short stature; to improve poor balance due to disproportionately short legs

Ana—to improve large-motor skills; to gain confidence in joining groups

3. Set goals

Nathan—to gain better balance and to be offered the chance to feel tall and big

Ana—to become a bit more adventurous, more sociable, and more comfortable with her body in space

4. Brainstorm: What group activities are suitable?

Nathan—physical activities that require stretching and balancing

Ana—noncompetitive experiences that require different kinds of motor planning and that allow her to proceed at her own pace while participating with her peers

5. Select an activity (e.g., an outdoor obstacle course)

6. Plan the activity (see "Planning an Outdoor Obstacle Course")

7. Implement the activity (see "Building an Obstacle Course")

8. Evaluate the activity

Nathan—Was he able to stretch sufficiently to climb the rungs and reach across the empty spaces between obstacles? Did he work on his balancing skills?

Ana—Was she willing and able to work through the course? Did she need a teacher's hand throughout? Did she interact with her peers?

Both—Did they do the whole course or did they skip some obstacles? Did they return to a favorite spot? Did they voluntarily repeat the whole course?

All—Did everybody have fun?

9. Refine the activity—and try again!

Planning an outdoor obstacle course

Select the site

An ideal site for an obstacle course is an open, flat, grassy area, removed from swings and ball fields. The site should not be so wide open that children may wander off or so distant from the storage area that lugging equipment to and fro becomes impractical. Other good sites are a corner of the blacktop playground or a classroom reserved for large-motor activities.

Plan the course

The goal of an obstacle course it to awaken the children's kinesthesia, or muscle sense. This is especially important for a child like Ana. The perfect course will engage as many motor skills as possible: balancing, alternating feet, crawling, climbing, somersaulting, scooting, sliding, ascending and descending inclines, leaping, jumping, pulling and reaching, and taking big steps. Mastering each obstacle requires motor planning. Motor planning involves eye-foot coordination as well as spatial awareness, an understanding of the relationship of one's body in space.

The simplest course—for the teacher to build and for the children to execute—runs in a great circle. It is linear in design. The first obstacle leads directly to the second, the second to the third, and, eventually, the last right back to the first. A logical order of obstacles will help the child understand the sequence and will keep the children moving, one after the other. (Not recommended are courses designed in a straight line, in a figure-eight, or in a radial pattern. In a straight line, children begin and end at a different point and tend to meander away when they have completed the course once. In a figure-eight, the children become confused when their paths cross in the middle. In a radial pattern, with many obstacles converging at the center, chaos prevails.)

Alternate the obstacles so that the children must vary both their body posture and their form of locomotion as they proceed from one challenge to the next. It is helpful to mutter prepositions to yourself as you work—*up, down, across, through, over, under, into,* and *around.*

Assemble the equipment

Be creative with permanent obstacles on the playground, turning landscape timbers into balance beams and tree stumps into stepping stones. The advantage of using obstacles that are stuck in the ground is not having to put them away.

As for portable equipment, get the best your budget can afford; quality is better than quantity. Use everything you've got, even if it isn't weatherproof. Just remember not to leave wooden pieces out in the rain. When you store the equipment, keep it together in an accessible spot. Store weatherproof aluminum pieces outside, lashed to a tree with a long chain and a strong lock.

The Suggested Equipment list on the next page suggests tried-and-true pieces of equipment, available through early childhood mail order catalogs.

Building an obstacle course

Begin at the beginning

A red traffic cone (A) marks the spot where the course begins and ends.

Obstacle #I—Up

The first obstacle is a walking board (B), sloping gently upward. The closest end rests on the ground; the far end is attached to a sawhorse (C). Some children, like Nathan, will zip up an incline with one fearless bound, while others, like Ana, ascend tentatively, testing the reliability of the board with every step.

Obstacle #2—Over

The second obstacle is straddling the sawhorse. Nathan will step blithely over it. Ana may crouch, grip the top rung of the sawhorse with both hands, and back carefully over it until she feels secure.

Obstacle #3—Down

The third obstacle is a descending walking board. Nathan will run or jump down in a series of bounds. Ana will walk cautiously or will sit, half sliding, half scooting to the bottom. There is no *one way*. The act of ascending and descending a sloping walking board can be scary. The receding and approaching ground beneath young children's feet challenges their relatively recent sense of equilibrium.

Obstacle #4—Up

Allow a couple of yards of clear ground so that their momentum will not send the children crashing into the next obstacle: the first of three nesting aluminum climbing bridges (D). Ascending the rungs encourages the use of alternate hands and feet, a valuable exercise for both Ana and Nathan.

Obstacle #5—Across

The fifth obstacle is an aluminum gangway (E), suspended between level rungs of the first and second climbing bridges. (Initially, the gangway should be level; subsequently, it can be slanted for a greater challenge.) If crossing the open rungs of the

Suggested Equipment

A—Red traffic cones

B—Walking board

C—Sawhorse

D—Aluminum climbing bridges, set of three in graduated sizes

E—Aluminum gangway

F—Tumbling mat

G—Plastic action hoops, set of 5 large hoops and 10 grooved hoop holders

H—Connecting tunnel and two panels

I—Barrel and barrel rack

J—Balance beam

K—Triangle set

L—Hollow wooden blocks

M—Rocking boat

N—Crawl tunnel

O—Huskylight blocks

P—Tent cover

These items can be obtained from early childhood resource distributors, such as those that exhibit at NAEYC's Annual Conference; collect catalogs and you will find just about everything you need.

gangway appears too difficult, lay a walking board over them. The disadvantage of a solid walkway, however, is that children tend to congregate on it, stopping the flow of traffic. Nathan particularly loves to pause on the gangway, waving and calling, "Hey, guys! Hey down there!"

Obstacle #6—Down

The next obstacle is the second aluminum bridge. The motor planning involved in getting down the rungs is a complicated business. Nathan prefers to leap from the gangway, eliminating the problem altogether. Ana, like most preschoolers, needs help to turn around so she can back down, facing the rungs.

Obstacle #7—Over

Next comes a tumbling mat (F). Children are inspired by a mat's resilience and gentle bounciness. Let them discover their favorite form of locomotion. They may somersault, roll, crawl, or run over the mat. They may leap up and fall down in an exaggerated heap. Ana likes to tiptoe here. Anything goes.

Obstacle #8—Through

After the mat comes an obstacle through which to crawl. Crawling is not only for babies; cross-lateral locomotion (whereby opposite arms and legs move forward at the same time) helps to integrate the left and right hemispheres of the brain. When the brain hemispheres are working smoothly together, the whole child functions better, often with noticeable improvements in social behavior, motor skills, and cognitive ability.

Plastic action hoops (G), secured vertically in specially grooved blocks, serve the purpose of a crawl-through obstacle. Hoops are colorful, versatile, and easy to store but are often knocked down by exuberant children. A sturdier piece of equipment that will invite children to get down on all fours is either a plastic tunnel secured between two panels (H), or a wooden barrel and barrel rack (I), treated for outdoor use.

Obstacle #9—Across

Two balance beams (J), wide side up and set parallel to each other, make a novel obstacle. A child who was developmentally delayed, both emotionally and physically, invented this side-by-side set-up because a single balance beam was too frustrating for her. Nathan finds the arrangement very amusing. He often remarks, "Two balance beams? That's so funny!"

Obstacle #10—Around

Weaving around a series of traffic cones is next. Set down five cones, about 18 inches apart, in a gentle S. To make a serpentine path for the children to follow, sprinkle flour on the ground beside the cones. Flour makes a good path because it is biodegradable, highly visible, and, unlike a rope, stays put. Ana thinks well of this obstacle, saying, "This is like Hansel and Gretel."

Obstacle #11—Up, Across, and Down

A teetering balance board is the next challenge. Devised by a four-year-old, this risky-looking obstacle provides another exercise that helps integrate the left and right brain hemispheres and thus improves motor and thinking skills.

Center a walking board atop a small wooden triangle (K), as if it were a seesaw. Where each end of the board hits the ground, place a hollow block (L); the blocks will reduce the board's slant.

First the child inches up the inclined board. Then he balances momentarily at the fulcrum as his shifting weight causes the board to level. Finally, he runs off the board as it tips downward to strike the block. Many children, like Ana, need a teacher's hand and will sigh with pride and relief when they return to terra firma. Other children, like Nathan, will want to stand astride the fulcrum and balance, unaided, forever.

Obstacle #12—Into

More hoops, secured horizontally in their grooved blocks, require another kind of balancing skill. A child must balance on one foot while raising the other foot high in order to step into each hoop. This is not easy for Nathan, but he likes to pretend he is stepping into a boiling cauldron, like the wolf in *The Three Little Pigs,* or into icy cold water, infested by sharks. "Yikes!"

Obstacle #13—Over

Getting over an inverted rocking boat (M) by stepping up and down the stairs is next.

Obstacle #14—Across

A single balance beam, wide side up, is a true challenge. Let the children cross it any way they can—walking as if on a tightrope, sidling, holding a teacher's hand, or with one foot on the ground and the other on the board.

Obstacle #15—Through

A metal crawl tunnel (N) is next. Its open sides and colorful rungs make it an appealing obstacle. Flat on the ground, it invites children either to shimmy forward on their backs, feet first, or to crawl through on their hands and knees. Later, raise the tunnel at one end to provide a challenge for either crawling up or sliding down. Nathan, of course, likes it at a rakish tilt.

Obstacle #16—Across

On their feet again, children walk across *stepping stones.* Position tree stumps, hollow blocks (O), or inverted milk cartons about four to six inches apart.

Obstacle #17—Under

The last obstacle is the third climbing bridge, placed sideways in the children's path so that they must crouch slightly to pass under it. Because an unattached climbing bridge may be unstable, throw a tent cover (P) or blanket over the rungs to dissuade children from climbing it. Ana likes to spend a cozy moment inside the covered bridge, where she can contemplate her next move.

End at the beginning

Having come full circle, the children meet the solitary red traffic cone that marks the beginning of the course—and they start all over again.

General guidelines

An obstacle course is addictive; we build one every day. Sure, it takes physical energy to carry wooden rocking boats from shed to playground, but letting the children help works well. To children, putting together a course is not work, but play. It builds muscles

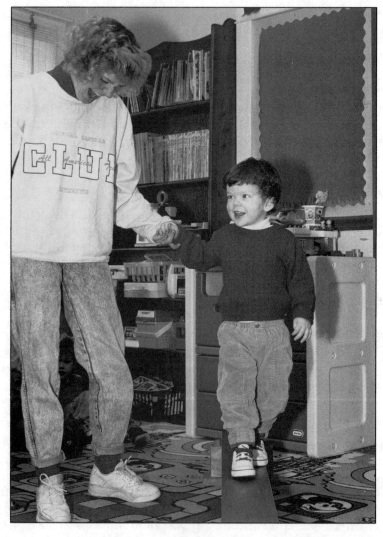

and channels energy. Because it requires teamwork and group interaction, it develops social skills. It encourages creative thinking about ways to use equipment—ways grown-ups wouldn't consider themselves. It strengthens problem-solving skills as children figure out how to incorporate their ideas into the master plan. It involves children as participants rather than spectators. It is, above all, glorious fun!

With the children's guidance I've learned to build a course neither so difficult that Ana needs a helping hand throughout nor so simple that Nathan considers it a big bore. Let the children tell you what they want; they know, whereas teachers can only guess.

It is important to be vigilant about safety. Sufficient space between obstacles and stability of equipment are imperative. Check the obstacles frequently to make certain they are secure. If you must leave the site, ask another teacher to take your place so that a responsible adult is always in attendance.

Avoid giving orders to the children. Do not, for example, insist that everyone do somersaults; the children won't like it, and neither will you.

Give your slow starters a little extra time before they leap into an obstacle course. Ana likes to watch for a while, to measure how the course is run. She digs her heels in and resists participating if she feels pushed or rushed. She gains confidence, however, if she feels that she can join in when she is good and ready. With gentle encouragement, shy children will participate, especially when a trusted teacher is right beside them. Soon the children will be able to repeat the course alone, as Ana does, shining with pleasure and crowing, "I did it all by myself!"

To keep the obstacle courses engaging, vary each one by adding and subtracting elements. One day it might be a *Shape Course*, emphasizing squares, triangles, or circles. A *Color-of-the-Day Course* is another variation. On Valentine's Day you may use only red plastic hoops and apply red arrows and hearts to the walking boards. A *Zigzag Course* provides a different challenge because changing direction is very hard. Sometimes set up the course indoors instead of outdoors. Sometimes it may become an integral part of enacting a nursery rhyme, such as *Jack and Jill*. Let the children try the course barefoot. Or backwards. Or with music. Variations are endless; no obstacle course design is written in stone.

Once the assembling is over, step back to watch and listen. Success is in the air, for everybody loves an obstacle course, each in a *different* way.

CAROL STOCK KRANOWITZ has been the music and creative movement teacher at St. Columba's Nursery School in Washington, D.C., since 1976.

Helping Whole Children Grow: Nonsexist Childrearing for Infants and Toddlers

Judith Leipzig

Ask a group of teachers about sex-role stereotyping in the earliest years and most will laughingly respond with "Boys in blue— girls in pink!" or "Trucks for boys—dolls for girls!"—knowing that they would not enforce such codes themselves. It is difficult for most of us to identify what might be some of the subtler links between the way we care for babies and toddlers and the limitations and problems experienced by adult men and women. So often it seems as if we interact with babies in response to the individual child, and most teachers would no sooner take a truck away from a toddler girl or steer a baby boy from a doll than they would dress each child, according to sex, in a pink or blue uniform. The general sense among most adults is that sex-role stereotyping begins in nursery school or later.

The research during the past few decades can provide us with a lot of food for thought. Most importantly, it may be surprising to learn that no study has conclusively identified any difference between male and female behaviors, activity levels, or interests at birth or in the first two years of life. Research has substantiated behavioral differences in males and females later in life, making it difficult to make a case for girls or boys behaving in a certain way because they're biologically programmed to do so. By the time sex differences do show up, much has happened to a child that could conceivably have influenced the development of gender typing.

Other research (Murphy, 1962; Moss, 1967; Fagot, 1973; Cherry, 1976) has shown that adults, even those concerned about sex-role stereotyping in later years, do handle male and female babies differently right from the start; and this probably contributes to the very diverse experiences boys and girls have with people, activities, and objects. This, in turn, feeds back into children's self-images, skills, and interests.

A number of studies (Seavey, 1975; Condry, 1976; Will, 1976) sought to discover if this differential handling was an unconscious response to actual sex differences. This research focused on adult interaction with infants and the adults' interpretation of babies' feelings and communications based on the *perceived* sex of the infant. In these studies, when adults were told that a baby was *male*, they were more likely to see him as sturdy, aggressive, big, angry, and so forth. The same child, when perceived as *female*, was described as delicate, sweet, tiny, frightened, and so forth. If the study was an interactional one, the adults were more likely to touch, smile at, and talk with the *female* baby, and to hand *her* a doll to play with, while the adults who interacted with the *same* child, but who were told that *he* was a boy, offered the child male stereotyped toys, such as a small train.

The creation of Project Beginning Equal

In 1982 the Pre-School Association of the West Side, Inc. (PAWS) approached the New York Community Trust with an idea. PAWS suggested setting up a program that would review the research in child development and sex-role stereotyping and proceed to develop a series of workshops to help parents and teachers of children under the age of three learn to identify some of the ways in which they pass along this damaging sex-role socialization. Little work had been done to translate this research into action, to identify how to become aware of and change some of our behaviors. The New York Community Trust decided to fund a joint two-year project to be conducted by PAWS and the Nonsexist Child Development Project of the Women's Action Alliance, Inc.—an agency with a substantial background in the development of nonsexist curriculum for older children. Out of this collaboration, Project Beginning Equal (BE): The Project on Nonsexist Childrearing for Infants and Toddlers was developed.

The project began with several months of observations and interviews in nine New York City infant/toddler child care centers. Team members had several tasks. First, they noted materials available in the rooms and who (boys and/or girls) was using them. Second, when team members entered the room for the first time, they immediately attempted to identify which children were male and which were female, noting which cues (e.g., dress, hairstyle) might be acting as a gender signal. Later, the observer checked her judgment with the teacher. The results of this exercise followed the pattern concluded by current research: team members could not guess what sex a child was unless one of several signs was apparent—girls sported ornaments and bright colors, while boys wore darker clothing and usually had what little hair they possessed parted on the side.

Arrivals and departures at the center were observed, since interactions between adults and children are often highlighted during these emotional times. In addition, individual observers randomly chose a child and described everything that child did for 15 minutes. The project made use of these observations in the development of workshops, including "Exploring One's Sex-Role Attitudes"; "Sex-Role Socialization—Adult Interactions with Infants and Toddlers"; "Identifying Conflicts and Developing Strategies for Change"; and "Analyzing Toys for Sex and Race Stereotyping." An additional follow-up workshop, focusing mainly on conflicts with other adults (spouses, other staff, relatives, etc.), was added.

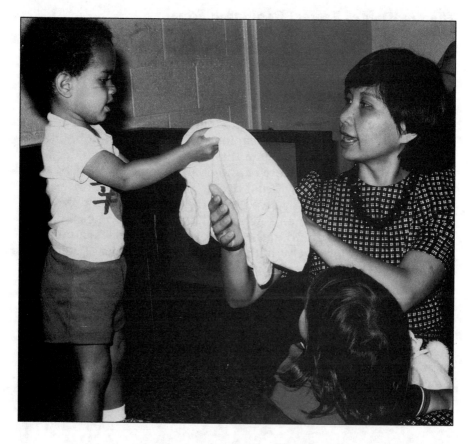

Implications of BE for early childhood programs

It is possible to take the material developed by Project BE and translate it into our work with children under the age of three in the classroom. Designing a curriculum for children of that age takes a special understanding of how infants and toddlers learn, as well as an awareness of what the real course of study is for very young children. The most important learning in the first years is finding out about the self: what one feels, what one can do, how one fits in, and what the world feels like pressed up against and funneled through the self. Without this grounding, all else must be less meaningful. In an educational setting, curriculum for infants and toddlers is anything a child feels or experiences that is put into a focused and responsive framework for that baby by the staff.

So much of what children learn about themselves and the world comes not through carefully planned activities but through the many repeated everyday encounters that make up a day. What research shows, and the Project BE observations corroborated, is that, in general, boys and girls have different experiences and are interacted with in distinct ways by adults, based not on actual individual differences, nor even as a result of differences in the child's style, but on the basis of unconscious assumptions made by teachers and parents. These assumptions about children's innate needs, abilities, styles, and futures alter teachers' behaviors drastically, so that girls are learning one curriculum and boys another.

Teachers who want to begin to think about developing their own nonstereotyping curriculum can start with the basic premise that the wider a child's range of experience, both with the self and with the outer world, the more likely he or she is to become a well-rounded person. Instead of taking trucks away from the boys, add experience for the boys in the doll corner. Instead of taking art projects away from the girls, add some exciting gross-motor play. Children need opportunities for exploring different kinds of relationships with people, materials, and activities. They need the chance to incorporate information about closeness *and* separateness, about assertiveness *and* cooperation.

Patterns in adult-child interactions

As the specialist in infant and parent development with the Project BE team, it was my job to review the 70-plus observations collected by the team members. These anecdotes suggested to me a number of patterns about adult-child interactions. It is important to note that these hypotheses are not the result of actual research but are questions and ideas gleaned from the observations that follow the path identified by actual research studies. As teachers, we can use these hypotheses to begin to view our own behavior with a more critical eye.

Two-year-old Luis and 20-month-old Alma are crying for their mothers. Two caregivers approach them warmly: "Hey, Luis honey," says the first. "Did you see the new red blocks we got for the block corner? Come on, let's go take a look." The other adult takes Alma in her arms, saying, "I know you're feeling sad because you're missing your mommy. She's gone to work, but she'll be back after lunch. It'll be okay. I'm gonna take good care of you."

This observation reflects the sense that boys were generally steered away from experiencing their feelings, while girls were supported in exploring theirs. Teachers encouraged boys to find something to do or play with when they were sad, but teachers talked to, cuddled, and articulated the girls' experiences for them. In the story above, Alma's caregiver is providing her with some very important information: Alma learns that the important adult both recognizes her feelings and respects them. She begins to put together a more coherent picture of her inner turmoil—among other things, Alma is learning that there are names for these feelings (sad and missing); there is a reason for them (mommy has gone away); and the occasion for the sadness has a limit (it will end after lunch). Luis, on the other hand, has his most intense emotional experience blanked out. It seems possible that this difference in handling could contribute to the difficulty many adult men experience in connecting with their feelings.

By 11 A.M. the floor of the child care center is strewn with the remains of some very intense playing. "Cleanup time," calls the teacher. "We've got to get ready to go outside. Here, Lucy, you can help me find all the red Legos, now all the blue ones. Can you put them in this box? Terrific, you're really doing a good job!" As the teacher works with 15-month-old Lucy, she glances over at a cluster of two-year-old boys who are already pulling their coats out of their cubbies. "Really, it's more trouble than it's worth to try to get the boys to help with cleanup."

In the BE samples, it appeared that teachers took for granted that girls should be learning to be aware of their environment and to take some responsibility in cleaning up, setting the table for lunch, and so forth. They devised interesting ways to help the girl toddlers begin to be socialized in this way. In contrast, they failed to pursue this area of curriculum with the boys. Those teachers who did call out a general announcement for cleanup usually did not give the boys the support and encouragement needed to develop skills in this area. Instead, boys were left to continue playing or to drift aimlessly. One wonders what connection this lack of social learning has with the general unawareness, lack of skill, and lack of personal responsibility that many adult men have when it comes to caring for their home environment.

Twelve-month-old Carla has been getting ready to walk on her own. This morning, with a look of great concentration, she struggles to take her first steps. She crows in triumph as she toddles toward the caregiver. "Oh, Carla! Don't you look pretty! Hey, cute thing— look at you strutting your stuff!" exclaims one caregiver. Another adult says, "Doesn't she look so sweet with those pretty lace panties wiggling along?"

Often girls were complimented on their appearance, boys on their achievements. Even when baby girls were achieving important milestones, it was their appearance that was commented on. In the example above, the responses of the caregivers, although warm and excited, were actually missing what the point of the experience was for this child. Instead of cheering on her first steps, exclaiming over her new motor abilities, her competence, or her maturity, the teachers emphasized for Carla how appealing, how accessible, and even possibly how sexy she was to others. A 12-month-old boy walking for the first time might have heard "Yay! Good walking! Look at that big guy—good for you!"—that is, the most salient aspect of his experience would have been noted. The thrust seems to be that boys are encouraged to do things as a response to their own inner drives, interests, and development, and that adults value the achievement in terms of its meaning for the child.

Again, we can think about the implications for later life. Many adult women struggle to identify what they actually want to achieve for themselves, since part of female socialization makes it difficult for women to see their own needs and interests separate from the desires and priorities of others. One could hypothesize that this turning of achievement into a chance to be attractive and pleasing to others might contribute to this facet of female development.

In one center, eight-month-old Brian begins to cry. Marian, a caregiver, picks him up and cuddles him, to no avail. She changes his diaper and offers him a bottle; these actions have no effect on the crying. Marian and her co-teacher become increasingly concerned, attempting one thing after another to figure out what might be going on, realizing that Brian's crying has meaning and is communicating a need that ought to be met.

In another center, 11-month-old Rebecca is urgently tugging at her special cuddly bear, which is caught under a rocking chair. Adult caregivers come and go, passing by Rebecca and the chair as they attend to their duties. Rebecca begins to whimper and crawls under the chair, looking for a way to retrieve her bear. She looks from bear to adult and back, whimpering loudly. Lois, a teacher, gives Rebecca an affectionate pat on the head and continues reading to another child. Finally Rebecca beings to howl loudly in frustration. "What's the matter with Rebecca?" asks Lois. "Oh, she's probably had it with being inside all morning," answers David. Rebecca is swooped up and carried to the door. No one has taken a moment to focus on what this child may be communicating.

These two anecdotes exemplify the way adults tend to miss the cues of preverbal girls more frequently than of preverbal boys. Teachers attempted to decode the communications and gestures of the infant boys more consistently in the Project BE observations; in fact, they often did not even notice that a baby girl had expressed a desire or need.

In addition, observers noted that male toddlers were allowed to wander around the room, generally able to follow their own internal schedules and interests, collecting important information about people and things as they cruised through space. Female toddlers, in contrast, were frequently interrupted in their explorations. The girls were more consistently required to curtail or interrupt their self-motivated activities to respond to the teacher's schedule or needs. In behavioral terms, it may look something like this: a little girl who is concentrating on the challenges of a shape-sorting box is interrupted from her work by a teacher who swoops the child up suddenly for a hug. In another illustration of this dynamic, a teacher decides it is time to change a girl's diaper or take her for a walk, and immediately acts on her decision, even though the girl toddler is engrossed in water play. The child is not permitted the few moments needed to feel a sense of completion. Baby girls were not responded to in ways that support the growth of a sense of personal effectiveness, a sense that one can order and cope with the environment. Adult women often have difficulty maintaining an image of themselves as effective individuals—as people who can decide on a goal, form a plan of action, and then *go for it.* Without this feeling, it's much harder to create a life of one's own.

The teacher is sitting on the floor with two little boys while they play with the Bristle Blocks. As the boys build, the teacher presents herself as a focusing and grounding presence by simply being there, commenting on their work, mentioning the colors, the textures, and the ideas. Over to the side, a girl toddler sits, watching all the activity wistfully, turning a single Bristle Block over and over in her hands.

Another group of BE observations seemed to point to the hypothesis that teachers view onlooking girls as participants. If a girl was watching an activity, teachers were much less likely to try to draw her into the activity, much less likely to help her have a hands-on experience, than they would be with a boy. Teachers usually interpret a boy's interest as an interest to be *doing* and help the child find his way into the activity. Girls miss some of those important learning experiences because teachers view the girls' observing as sufficient participation. In the story above, the boys were learning (to name a few concepts) to work together, to develop their ideas, to concentrate, information about spatial relationships, fine-motor skills, and about color. The experiences that children have in the early years are the foundational blocks upon which later learning and competencies are built. Those adults who have had the opportunity to develop basic skills and collect this information early on are better equipped to learn what they need in order to function in our complex and demanding world. If little girls are shortchanged in this respect, adult women may suffer.

Conclusion

Since *we* are the most important tools of our curriculum concepts, it is mandatory for us to observe ourselves, to review our personal assumptions about children, and to repeatedly help each other shake free of these biases. The teachers that Project BE observed were for the most part caring and responsible people; but like all of us, they were often acting on unconscious assumptions that we have all been taught. Much more important than what we

Checklist for Self-Observation

Before you start to make changes, take a week to begin to observe yourself in your interactions with children. The following questions may be helpful in organizing your observations:

1. Look around the room several times a day. Are boys only playing with gross-motor toys and blocks? Are girls only in the housekeeping corner or at the fine-motor table? Do you personally spend little time in areas traditionally labeled for the other sex?

2. Observe the way you handle times of emotional stress for boys and for girls. Are you unconsciously distracting boys from their feelings while you give girls support for and language to describe their distress?

3. Notice what happens during cleanup times. Who helps? Does your staff try to think of imaginative ways to involve most of the children who are old enough to participate?

4. Watch carefully and note repeatedly the way you talk. Are you aware of the language you use with children? What do you focus on to praise about little girls? about little boys? Observe yourself carefully to see what you applaud, or even comment on, and what the underlying messages might be that you are sending with the words you choose.

5. Think before you interrupt any child. Ask yourself: Is it necessary? What is the child experiencing right now? How can I give him or her time to complete this and still get my work done?

6. Compare your responses to a few of the baby girls and a few of the baby boys to see if there are different patterns of care. Are you noticing the communications of preverbal girls? When you do notice them, do you put effort into deciphering their meaning? It may be helpful for staff members to take turns sitting on the sidelines and trying to write down more objective observations since it's often easier to notice behaviors when one is unencumbered and uninvolved.

7. Take a look at how the children are engaged in their play. Do all children actively participate in what's going on in the room? How often are there children sitting on the periphery of an activity for long periods of time, showing interest but not able to actually join in? What sex are they?

directly say to the infants and toddlers in our care are these many daily personal interactions and the messages they impress on the individual child. When a child receives messages—either directly through words and gestures or less directly through assumptions and fantasies adults have about the child—that child is absorbing a picture of what is possible, what is permissible, and what is to be. When we talk about sexist childrearing, we're talking about something that goes far beyond isolated and superficial pieces of behavior—far beyond dressing girls in pink and boys in blue. This kind of experience becomes a lens through which children will see the world and themselves.

As educators of very young people who are in the midst of creating their selves and their futures, we must think about what kinds of raw materials we are providing them. Each child should have the support, the attention, and the experiences that will help that child grow to be a competent, well-rounded, loving person—one who has a clear picture of her or his self, one who is able to cooperate and to work on her or his own, and one who is able to both give and receive support and nurturing. As teachers of infants and toddlers, we should be doing everything in our power to support the development of individuals who will be capable of leading rich and balanced lives.

References

Cherry, L., & Lewis, M. (1976). Mothers of two year olds: A study of sex differentiated aspects of verbal interaction. *Merrill-Palmer Quarterly*, l3.

Condry, J., & Condry, S. (1976). Sex differences: A study of the eye of the beholder. *Child Development*, 47.

Fagot, B.I. (1973). Sex-related stereotyping of toddler behaviors. *Developmental Psychology*, 9.

Maccoby, E.E., & Jacklin, D.N. (1974). *The psychology of sex differences*. Stanford, CA: Stanford University Press.

Moss, H.A. (1967). Sex, age and state as determinants of mother-infant interaction. *Merrill-Palmer Quarterly, 13.*

Murphy, L.B. (1962). *The widening world of childhood*. New York: Basic Books.

Seavey, C.A., et al. (1975). Baby X: The effect of gender labels on adult responses to infants. *Sex Roles, 1.*

Will, J.A., et al. (1976). Maternal behavior and perceived sex of infant. *American Journal of Orthopsychiatry, 46.*

Women's Action Alliance, Inc. and the Pre-School Association, Inc. (1983). *Beginning equal: A manual about nonsexist childrearing for infants and toddlers*. New York: Women's Action Alliance.

JUDITH LEIPZIG is a specialist in early childhood and parent development who has worked with young children and their families in a wide variety of settings. She is an early childhood consultant in the New York [City] area.

Lost in a Distant Land: The Foreign Child's Dilemma in Child Care

Athol B. Packer, Sharon C. Milner, and Marion H. Hong

An Asian mother and her three-year-old son, who speak very little English, approach the center's front door. When the child's mother encourages him to enter, his whine turns into a loud wail. Some children stop playing and stare at him. A teacher stops her planning work and tries to draw the child into the classroom activities. After 30 minutes this young mother is still by the door; whenever she turns and tries to walk away, her child follows and clings to her leg.

For a minute, try to put yourself in a similar situation. Imagine yourself in a foreign country where you don't speak the language and the natives do not speak English. In such a predicament you might feel considerable anxiety and discomfort. Just satisfying your basic needs—getting a drink of water or finding a bathroom—can cause problems. You feel lost and disoriented, cut off from natural means of communication. Those who have traveled in a foreign country can certainly relate to these circumstances.

Non-English-speaking children placed in a child care center face much the same situation. They are in a foreign country, a land of giant adults who speak a strange language. For many of these children, this is their first separation from their parents. To help these children adjust to new experiences, it is necessary to become more sensitive to their particular needs. Foreign families have special problems adjusting to child care. This chapter describes a program developed to aid foreign children, their parents, and their teachers.

Thirty-three three- and four-year-old children from foreign countries were enrolled for full-time child care at the University of Florida's Baby Gator Educational Research Center for Child Development in August 1986. The children and their families came from

20 countries, including Brazil, Venezuela, Costa Rica, Korea, China, Iran, Egypt, India, Israel, Poland, Malaysia, Bangladesh, Cameroon, and South Africa. The high percentage of foreign children results from our center being located on the University of Florida campus. Our student population includes a substantial number of married foreign students with children. The majority of preschool centers in the United States might typically have only a few non-English-speaking children from other countries.

Thirty-five foreign children out of a total of 105 in a child care center—what are the implications for children, parents, and staff?

• Separation anxiety of young foreign children is heightened by their inability to communicate adequately with peers and teachers.

• Parents, especially mothers of young foreign children, have special needs and concerns that need to be addressed, such as lack of confidence and security about the center and, perhaps, reluctance to use a new language.

• Teachers experience stresses and frustrations in working with these families and their particular needs in addition to all of their other responsibilities.

Lost in a Distant Land: The Foreign Child's Dilemma/Packer, Milner, and Hong 43

How are the children affected?

Foreign children may experience anxiety and fear beyond that of other children because they lack the language skills to communicate their needs. For example, the child may say, "I need to go to the bathroom" in her language. A teacher not knowing the child's language might think that the child is asking for a drink of water or to go outside and play. It can be very frustrating to the child not to be understood. Fortunately these young children pick up nonverbal cues from English-speakers that eliminate many communication fears, and they are also quick to use their own body language to fill in the gaps. Because everything may be so different in the center, it can be especially difficult for these children to develop a sense of belonging.

What are the parents feeling?

The foreign parent may feel as lost and lonely in our country as her child does. She may be anxious about the welfare of her child because she is unable to talk easily about her concerns. She may even be hesitant to try asking the staff about the program or what her child does all day in the center. Even when the staff provides her a schedule of the daily activities, terms such as *free play*, *cubbie*, and *circle time* may be unfamiliar to her.

Foreign parents who place their children in a child care center may also be suffering from separation anxiety. The staff can comfort them by saying, "It's okay to feel bad and a little anxious when you are leaving your child for the first time." Just recognizing and acknowledging that you understand their feelings about leaving their child may be all that is needed to relieve their anxiety. They can also be encouraged to stay and observe; some of what may be difficult to communicate verbally can be learned by just watching what goes on in the program. Efforts to help parents deal with their feelings will pay big dividends for parents and children and will make the center's work easier and more effective.

What is the impact on the teachers?

At the beginning of the school year, teachers are faced with a multitude of tasks to accomplish. Lesson plans must be prepared. Teaching materials must be gathered. The room must be organized. New children—in fact, all children—must be welcomed and helped to feel comfortable and secure. Teachers must also communicate with parents to help them feel secure. These teacher tasks can seem overwhelming. Add to this the particular needs of several non-English-speaking children and their parents, and teachers may feel that it's more than they can handle. Teachers, as well as the children and their parents, need help in adjusting to working together in the program.

What can be done to help the children adjust?

The child care center has to take an active role in developing and implementing strategies to aid the adjustment of foreign parents and children. The following strategies have worked in our center.

Teachers are encouraged to maintain eye contact when talking to non-English-speaking children and to be aware of the children's nonverbal body language. Because words for objects and actions that can be displayed or demonstrated are much easier for children to learn, teachers are encouraged to speak slightly slower and to use gestures and visual cues.

A list of common terms and functioning words that children frequently use in a child care program was compiled by the teachers and the research assistant. The terms are translated into Spanish, Chinese, and Korean—the languages representing the majority of non-English-speaking children enrolled. (It is suggested that your program provide translations into other languages spoken by families in your center.) A brochure containing this list is given to foreign parents when they enroll their children. Parents are encouraged to talk about these words at home so that they become familiar to the child. Several other familiar words and phrases such as *share*, *What is your name?*, *My name is . . .*, and *Thank you* are often found to be important.

It is also helpful for teachers to try to communicate with children in their native language; even just a few words in a child's language can be comforting. Cassette tapes and simple versions of foreign language phonetic transcriptions are made for teachers to learn the pronunciation of the terms in the child's language.

When new foreign children arrive in school, teachers are encouraged to provide a *bilingual buddy* to add to the children's security. If there is another child who speaks the same language as the new child, this bilingual friend can help as both translator and person to identify with to help ease the transition.

Guidelines for parents

Sometimes foreign parents are not aware that they are able to participate in local parent education classes, or they may not know about local services, such as the public library and the health clinic. Some mothers fear that their English is not fluent enough for them to take advantage of these services. This makes them reluctant to become involved in the community or to join the center's parental involvement program. Parents may also be unsure of what will help their children adjust and learn to communicate. Our brochure includes guidelines for parents to enhance their children's language and social adjustment:

• Encourage children to play with English-speaking children to enhance their language development.

• Encourage children to watch selected television programs ("Mr. Rogers," "Captain Kangaroo," "Sesame Street") to enrich their social background.

• Teach children basic safety rules:
  Beware of strangers.
  Only take medicines and food from mom, dad, or teachers.
  Keep small objects out of eyes, ears, and nose.
  Stay out of the street.
  Use words, not hitting, to solve problems.

• Check out children's books from the library:
  Going to Day Care by Fred Rogers (New York: G.P. Putnam Sons, 1985)
  I Can Build A House by Shigeo Watanabe (New York: Putnam Publishing Group, 1982)
  The Other Bone by Ed Young (New York: Harper and Row, 1984)
  Naptime by Gylbert Coker (New York: Delacorte Press, 1978)
  Geraldine's Blanket by Holly Keller (New York: Greenwillow Books, 1984)
  Whistle For Willie by Ezra Jack Keats (New York: The Viking Press, 1964)
  Snow by Isao Sasaki (New York: The Viking Press, 1980)
  A Tasting Party by Jane Belk Moncure (Chicago: Children's Press, 1982)
  The Very Hungry Caterpillar by Eric Carle (New York: Philomel Books, 1982)

• Check out story tapes from the library (in both English and your own language).

• Read to children in your native language.

• Become involved in your child's school as a teacher supporter or by helping with a special project.

• Participate in local parenting groups or English classes.

Guidelines for teachers

Teachers and children will do best when the atmosphere is relaxed and nonthreatening. Body language can take care of many basic communications, and teachers need to remind themselves that children will learn English quickly and naturally.

When developing learning activities, teachers should draw on the children's family and cultural backgrounds and personal interests. High-interest, fun activities such as finger plays and songs appeal to children across language barriers. Good illustrations help children understand the activity even though they may not comprehend all of the words they hear.

Classroom displays including objects or art familiar to the child, familiar foods at snack, and a favorite story all help the child feel that he belongs.

International potluck dinners can enhance the multicultural awareness of all of the children and their families.

A foreign parents' orientation meeting can help parents and teachers get to know each other better. Teachers can learn about parents' expectations for their children in the program, and parents can find out about the program's philosophy. In the past, parents have expressed appreciation for such special interest and concern. This orientation provides an opportunity for parents to express their concerns, thereby building their confidence and feeling of security about the center. When parents demonstrate this confidence, their children appear to adjust more easily and feel more secure in the program.

Common Terms Used in Child Care

eat	sit down	wake-up time
hungry	hold hands	pick-up time
water	toy	good touches/warm fuzzy
lunch time	cubbie	go to the bathroom/potty
snack time	telephone	wash hands
happy	free play	go inside
sad	cleanup time	go outside
quiet	rug time/story time	come here
listen	activity time	sick/I do not feel well
look	naptime	
hurt		

Conclusion

In American society, many cultures actively function within and alongside the mainstream. A sensitive caregiver will recognize this and provide these children with security and a comfortable setting. Furthermore, children in general will benefit from this multicultural involvement. We are excited about the results of our program, and we believe that these strategies can act as a model and a catalyst for the development of related child care programs. These strategies can facilitate better adjustment of foreign parents and children in the present and deeper international understanding in the future.

If you are interested in receiving a copy of the "Words Children Need at Preschool" brochure for parents and teachers of young bilingual children mentioned in this article, send a self-addressed, stamped envelope to Athol Packer, College of Education, 2207 Norman Hall, University of Florida, Gainesville, FL 32611.

ATHOL PACKER is professor emeritus at the University of Florida, Gainesville.

At the time of this book's original publication, SHARON MILNER was on leave from her position as director of Baby Gator and was teaching at the American School in Amsterdam, Holland.

MARION HONG is a speech therapist in the St. Tammany Parish, Louisiana, school system.

Guidelines for Helping Non-English-Speaking Children Adjust and Communicate

Karen Miller

• Build trust

The child needs you now. You are his *safe place*. As much as is practical, make yourself available for special holding. Although the child may not understand your words, he will understand eye contact, smiles, and reassuring touches. Once the child feels safe, he will begin to venture out, but you are definitely the starting point.

• Learn key words

Learn some key words and phrases in the child's language. Ask parents how the child will tell you she needs to go to the bathroom, she's tired, she's hungry, and other needs.

• Be a good language model

Speak slowly and clearly in a normal tone of voice. Use complete sentences. Extend single-word utterances of the child: When he says, "Shoes," say, "Yes, I see you have new red shoes on today."

• Build receptive language

Children will be able to understand things you say to them long before they will be able to say words or express themselves to you in words. This is receptive language, or understanding.

Talk a lot. Describe what you are doing and what the child is doing. Talk to the child as though he understands you, and then help him understand you by helping him do what you are talking about. "Masafumi, it's time to go to the table to eat lunch." Then take him by the hand, lead him over to the table, and sit down with him.

• Encourage productive language

Young children's brains are programmed to absorb language. They will pick up English very quickly. Often the first words a child says out loud are the social words: *hi, good morning, 'bye, thank you;* also *yes, no,* and *okay.* Encourage all of the children to say "Hi" or "Good morning" when other children arrive in the morning. Always say "Please" and "Thank you." You will be surprised how quickly these words come, and with what pride.

• Try to understand nonverbal communication

Read the child's nonverbal communication and supply the words. The child points to the pitcher and grunts. "Oh, you want more juice? I'll be glad to pour you some juice." You are acting as an interpreter for the child, connecting useful words to feelings. "Maria is sad because she can't find her hat."

• Encourage interactions

As the child builds a sense of trust with you, help her interact with other children. This will not only help her social adjustment, it will provide her with opportunities to hear English and to practice.

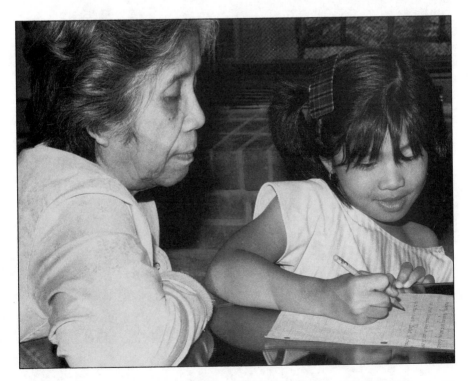

• Read books together

Read books that are familiar to the child over and over. Wordless picture books are valuable, as are stories with predictable outcomes and repetitive patterns.

• Listen and dance to music

Music touches us in a way all people understand. An inconsolable child might be comforted by some gentle singing from you. Songs with repeated phrases are good to use. "Ee-ei-ee-ei-o" is easy to master and fun to sing. Singing is much easier than talking because the words usually come out slower and are more predictable; it's good practice for productive language.

• Provide open-ended activities

Just like all other children, your non-English-speaking children will need many experiences of success to develop a feeling of self-worth. Try to arrange many open-ended, creative experiences for the child. Provide interesting materials, and anything the child comes up with is fine. Using play dough, water play, easel painting, manipulative play, and dramatic play are ideal open-ended activities, and they provide many concrete opportunities for language as well.

• Use appropriate discipline techniques

Whatever the child's culture or language, the discipline needs are the same. Children need firm, gentle guidance and consistent limits. Sometimes children will pretend not to understand your reprimands long after they really do understand. Remember that the nonverbal messages of a discipline situation are always understood, so make your tone of voice and facial expression match your words. If a child takes a toy from another child, simply get down on the child's level, hold her shoulders, look into her eyes, and say firmly, "No, that's not okay." Use the same techniques you use with the other children of praising good behavior and redirecting unacceptable behavior.

• Let the children teach

Encourage the child to teach you and the other children some words in his language. Make a book using these new words. Use the child's language and culture to redo the housekeeping corner. Let the child teach a song or a game. Learn to count in her language. Invite the parents to share a tradition or a cooking lesson, to read a familiar book in their language, or to share a different clothing style.

• Exchange pictures

Ask parents to bring in pictures of their family, family celebrations, former home, and other family situations to display in the center. Send pictures of you and the children home with the child. Such photo exchanges foster a sense of belonging.

KAREN MILLER has worked as a teacher for Head Start and as director of four different child care centers, and has held national positions in staff and administrative training and curriculum development for two major child care organizations. The author of Things to Do with Toddlers and Twos, More Things to Do with Toddlers and Twos, Ages and Stages, *and* The Outside Play and Learning Book, *Karen has also co-authored early childhood curriculum books and is the publisher of* Caring for the Little Ones, *a newsletter for people who work with infants and toddlers.*

Recognizing Giftedness in Early Childhood Settings

Donna Garnett Chitwood

Three-year-old Justin had been the subject of discussion among the teachers in his preschool for several months. He was a highly verbal, active, curious child who spent hours conversing with the adults in the room, but he rarely interacted with age peers. Activity times that were relatively unstructured were appealing to him, but he never seemed to pay attention in circle time. He would lie on the floor, rolling back and forth, playing with his fingers or clothing, looking around at everything but the teacher, and even sometimes humming softly to himself.

On one particular day one of his teachers sat down to observe the circle and Justin so that she could better talk to his parents about his behavior problems. She carefully recorded his behavior and the activities going on in the group interaction.

Several hours after circle time, the teacher had an opportunity to discuss with Justin the events and circumstances of the group activity earlier in the day. Not expecting a knowledgeable response, she nevertheless proceeded to ask the youngster about his experience. First she asked him to tell her about the circle time. In response he recounted the story that had been read and sang a 10-verse song that had been introduced for the first time that day. She then asked him what he was doing while the teacher was talking, to which he replied, "Listening."

Taking her investigation a step further, the teacher queried, "What were the other children doing during circle today?" Justin responded by describing where each of the 15 other children had been sitting, what they had said to the teacher and to each other, who got in trouble, who didn't sing, and so on. In utter awe, his teacher concluded that the parent conference had best focus on his exceptional abilities and how to better accommodate those abilities for his optimum development.

Justin's story is indicative of the nature of some gifted children who exhibit a different learning style from the mainstream of normal children. It was not until three years later that it was discovered that Justin had auditory processing problems and that his unusual way of *listening* was his way of compensating. Fortunately his preschool teacher had taken the time to observe and try to understand his behavior instead of just immediately categorizing him as a problem and punishing him for his *acting out.*

Tanisha was a charming little four-year-old girl. She loved coming to school and joyfully went about the business of doing all of the planned activities and then spending time in the dramatic play area, directing her friends in elaborate dramas. She enjoyed creative art and spent hours drawing and painting her representations of the world.

Soon her teacher began to notice that she was writing words to go along with her artwork—not just three- and four-letter-words but more descriptive ones like pepperoni pizza *and* acrimonious. *It was also becoming apparent that Tanisha was reading—as her dramatic play turned toward playing school and she gathered her friends around to read stories to them.*

Tanisha's exceptional abilities are easier to spot in the early childhood setting because they deviate so obviously from the normal developmental expectation and because they deviate in such a positive manner. For most teachers she is a delight, and very little has to be done with her because she is compliant and pleasant.

The dangerous aspect of Tanisha's case is that, as a girl, she is likely to be socialized to hide her giftedness by the time she is in

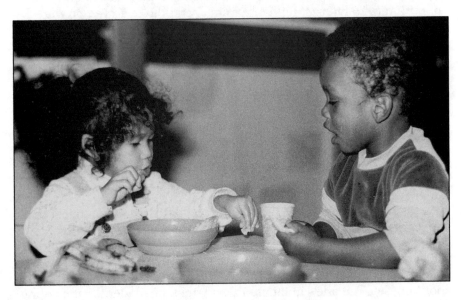

third grade. Much support for Tanisha and encouragement to not go underground will be necessary in the early grades. Her parents will need encouragement to pursue appropriate educational experiences for their daughter. There will be the temptation to sit back and accept her schooling experience because she will do well—so well, in fact, that she will disguise those abilities that threaten her acceptance by peers and teachers.

Another type of giftedness that is difficult to identify in the early childhood setting is the type that is buried within the exterior of an introverted, withdrawn child. This child's capabilities are difficult to observe because he or she doesn't readily verbalize perceptions of the world. This child might even be classified as *socially imma-ture* because he doesn't relate easily to his peers and prefers adult conversation over playing with his agemates.

Mario was just such a child. In the year that he had been in pre-school, he still didn't enthusiastically demand his turn during sharing time, and he still needed half an hour or more to warm up to the situation each day. During free play he usually chose soli-tary activities from the manipulative or science areas or followed one of the teachers around, engaging her in conversation. The teachers often remarked that he was 3 years old going on 30, yet in parent conferences his social immaturity was always the topic of discussion.

The summer when he was four, the preschool offered a special workshop for young gifted children. At his parents' insistence he was screened for the class, and through the skilled assessment made by the evaluating teacher, Mario was identified in the highly gifted range. During the summer workshop Mario had ample opportunity to interact with other children who operated on the same level as he did. There were very loose time constraints, so that there was still plenty of time to be involved after he had taken his normal warm-up time.

That summer he developed a special relationship with two other children as they constructed a river system in the sand pit, com-plete with terraces, logging camp, and dams. The teacher was amazed when one day she overheard a conversation among the three young engineers as they discussed the premise behind hydraulic energy! When allowed the time he needed to trust the environment and ensured that he had other children to relate to on his own cognitive level, Mario didn't look so immature.

As may be seen by these three examples, giftedness is manifest in a variety of ways. As with any other exceptional learning need, the earlier such need is identified, the better chances are that the child will get and respond to appropriate stimulation. As with all young children, a primary concern is the development of a healthy attitude about oneself and one's abilities. Taking the time to identify the young gifted child and trying to accommodate his or her special learning needs is absolutely critical to the development of that healthy attitude.

Identifying characteristics of gifted preschoolers

The first step in identification is to listen to the parents. Interestingly, studies show that when given specific criteria, parents are the best identifiers of their child's giftedness. Parents have observed their child's development over time and have usually built a safe enough environment for the child to exhibit her special abilities. Early childhood teachers can assist parents by becoming aware themselves of the characteristics of the young gifted child.

The Silverman/Waters Checklist for Identifying Giftedness provides a good guide for recognizing the characteristics associated with giftedness. These include the following:

• **Good problem-solving abilities**—may be problems involving things, people, or events.

• **Rapid learning ability**—for some things the child may pick up the relevant elements after hearing or seeing one demonstration. This child will be bored with the repetition typical of most preschool programs.

• **Extensive vocabulary**—uses language with great facility to describe and process the environment. Three-year-old Jesse astounded his teachers by explaining the big bang theory of the creation of the universe after the group had sung a song about 10 little rockets.

• **Good memory**—is able to remember events from months or even years before. Lisa once surprised her mother by asking if she could have a piñata for her birthday like the one Brian had for his party. Brian's party had been more than a year earlier, and Lisa had been only 18 months old when she had watched the piñata breaking.

• **Long attention span**—especially for things that he or she finds of great interest. Some gifted children can work for hours at a specific task in which they are interested.

• **Sensitivity**—may get feelings hurt easily or may be exceptionally tuned in to others' nonverbal communications.

• **Compassion for others**—may exhibit an unusual sensitivity to other adults, children, or animals. At four-and-a-half years old, Austin listened intently as the newscaster explained how a baby chimpanzee's heart had been transplanted into a very ill newborn human baby. He then turned to his mother and said, "That means that the baby chimpanzee died." Before she could respond, he tearfully queried, "Why is it okay for a baby human to live and a baby chimpanzee to die?"

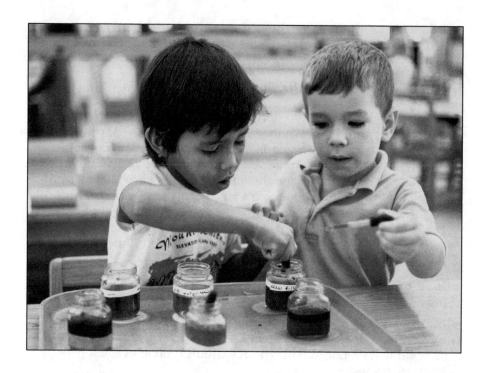

• **Perfectionism**—not necessarily in all areas, but in performance areas, may be reluctant to take risks for fear of failing.

• **High degree of energy**—may have considerably less need for sleep than other children; possibly dropped naps during early toddlerhood.

• **Preference for older companions**—enjoys the challenge of relating to older children and adults.

• **Wide range of interests**—usually interested in a great variety of subjects from dinosaurs to politics to trees and more.

• **Excellent sense of humor**—because of an advanced intellectual capacity, is able to see the absurdity of life, and particularly enjoys play on words.

• **Early or avid reading ability**—may actually become a self-taught reader at three or four years of age, or at least show a marked interest in being read to even from infancy.

• **Ability in puzzles, mazes, or numbers**—shows unusual ability in working difficult puzzles at an early age, or, like Mark, is able to add and subtract two-digit numbers by the age of five and has a fascination with the notion of negative numbers.

• **At times seems mature for age**—may have areas of development that almost seem delayed by comparison to intellectual ability, but on the whole seem exceptionally mature. Jessica could actually be left in charge of a small group of children if the teacher had to leave the room for a few moments.

• **Perseverance**—in areas of interest the child may continue with a project that is unusually difficult and frustrating. Theresa worked for several days to complete a sewing project that she had designed. Her four-year-old fingers had a difficult time matching the designs of her thoughts.

Children who display 10 of the 16 characteristics are very possibly gifted.

Testing for giftedness

The second step in identification is to assist the parents in locating the appropriate type of testing (if necessary). In many states special educational experiences for gifted children are not available until third grade. However, as with any special learning need, it is vital to have a clear picture of the situation as early as possible. Testing and assessment conducted by a trained professional can contribute greatly to a better understanding of the child. It is preferable that such assessment include an individual intelligence test, observations, and interviews with the parents.

For some parents, going through the testing procedure will ease their minds and help give perspective to the frustrations they have felt about parenting this special child. Although most parents of identified gifted preschoolers are initially pleased with the testing outcome, they very quickly become almost depressed about the burden of parenting a special-needs child. Support groups for parents and other opportunities to discuss their feelings and frustrations are especially beneficial at this time.

Providing appropriate learning experiences

Lastly, it is important that the child have the most appropriate experiences possible while still in the preschool environment.

• The young gifted child needs the opportunity to interact with other children who are at the same cognitive level; therefore, a mixed-age grouping can be especially beneficial for these children.

• The curriculum should allow for multilevel response and be challenging in a variety of ways. The young gifted child (as any other preschooler) does not need to spend hours completing workbook pages. A more appropriate approach is to provide more exploratory types of experiences with ample time to delve deeper into areas of special interest. Programs that focus on individualized planning and discovery models will be particularly suitable for the gifted child.

• As with all young children, focus on self-concept should be primary. The teacher must offer a safe environment in which the gifted child is able to overcome some of the perfectionism that accompanies giftedness and be able to try new experiences. Forcing the child to try something new will not be helpful; patience and sensitivity as to the conditions under which the child will try will be helpful. Providing an environment where right answers are not expected but where many possible answers exist will also be more appropriate.

• It is critical that the child's social immaturities not become a penalizing factor to his cognitive abilities. Preventing an extremely bright child from entering kindergarten because he is not ready socially may only make that gap seem larger in the future.

• Gifted children are rarely gifted in all areas, and the discrepancies between cognitive development and physical development are often sources of great frustration as the three-year-old body refuses to accomplish what the five-year-old mind conceptualizes. Adults must provide encouragement without placing adult standards on the products created, and adults can show short cuts over some difficult areas. For example, the adult can write down the creative story told by the youngster rather than insisting that she laboriously write her own words. Another option might be to show her how to work a tape recorder so she can record her own story.

Working with gifted children in the early childhood years can be a gratifying experience for teachers. It is critical, however, that teachers recognize that giftedness comes in many different forms and that not all of those children's achievements will look like Tanisha's. The different needs of all young children must be considered, and appropriate experiences must be facilitated to accommodate those individual differences.

For further reading

Karnes, M.B., & Johnson, L.J. (1989). Training for staff, parents, and volunteers working with gifted young children, especially those with disabilities and from low-income homes. *Young Children, 44*(3), 49–56.

Kitano, M.K. (1989). The K–3 teacher's role in recognizing and supporting young gifted children. *Young Children, 44*(3), 57–63.

Wolfle, J. (1989). The gifted preschooler: Developmentally different, but still 3 or 4 years old. *Young Children, 44*(3), 41–48.

DONNA GARNETT CHITWOOD is deputy director of Colorado Governor Roy Romer's Office of Policy and Initiatives. She oversees Families and Children Initiatives, Colorado 2000 Education Initiative, Communities for a Drug-free Colorado, First Impressions, and the Housing and Homeless Coordinating Council.

Exploring Diversity Through the Arts

Interviews with Jimena Lasansky and Richard Lewis
by Susan Epeneter
and an interview with Bob Blue
by Candace Chang

Question: *Poetry, storytelling, music, movement, dance—what can these different art forms contribute to a discussion of diversity?*

Answer: *Each can be used to broaden children's views and understandings of the world and its inhabitants. Artists involved in working with children in three different art forms were asked a series of questions regarding how the arts can be used to broaden children's perceptions of the world at large and the people, both like and unlike themselves, who inhabit that world. Each artist also offered suggestions for early childhood teachers in working to accomplish understanding and acceptance in children.*

*　　*　　*

Jimena Lasansky*: My focus is on dance, but my ultimate goal, of course, is not to create a multitude of dancers but to help children communicate issues they have within themselves. The beauty of dance is that dance is a universal way to communicate. In dance, in movement, in gesture, there are feelings. I can sit with a group and say, "Tell me something with your hands or with your fingers." Children immediately make associations; using gestures is a universal language.

Dance can be used with children within the same class who cannot communicate verbally for a multitude of reasons, either because of a physical or emotional handicap or because of a for-

---

**Jimena Lasansky is a professional dancer and choreographer and part-time professor of dance at the University of Maine in Augusta. She currently tours extensively, performing and conducting master classes and creative movement workshops for children and adults.*

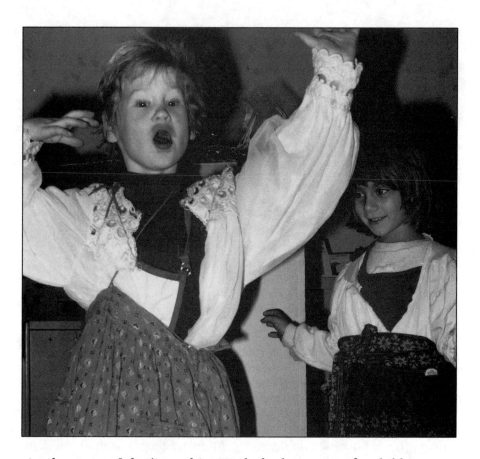

eign language. I don't need to speak the language of a child to understand what that child is trying to say to me. A child can simply toss his head to one side or the other, or lift her hand a little bit behind her back or head, and I know that he or she is slightly uncomfortable with what's going on. To the teacher, body language is very important. The more I communicate through the language of the body, as opposed to the word, the more it will help the child communicate to me through the body.

I have a fabulous opportunity to show the children how each of them is capable of and responsible for looking into any particular image and coming up with his or her own feeling. I realize that each of those children will come up with a different image, a different dance—and they will be attracted to different movements to accompany that dance. They'll be lured by a certain poem that will help describe that feeling. They'll look at each other and realize that, in reality, they were all inspired by a single image, like a shell from the ocean; yet the dances that they finally say, or speak, or move, will be very, very different. And yet, each one is valid.

That validity is extremely important because, generally, we have right and wrong, black and white. Validation is one way of helping the children realize that there's a very large spectrum of possibility. I think that most children instinctively realize that; but there's the fear of letting it out, fear of being wrong. We're so educated for right and wrong.

Once we get to the point where the children trust their own imagination and trust that within them they have their own substantial vocabulary to speak through movement, then comes the lovely area where we start focusing, harnessing that energy toward something specific that we want to say.

Children have a tremendous sense of imagination. Given a safe environment in which to play with that imagination, they're simply amazing; they're very deep. It's not so much that they become inhibited with age; rather, they become more inhibited as they hear from the world around them that certain things are not right. A child learns that if a is the problem, then b is the answer. Often children do not learn that if a is the problem, then b, c, d, e, and anything else they might come up with may possibly be a solution.

As they grow older children learn that there is an answer, rather than that there is the possibility of an answer. They should be learning that there is a process by which we come to a solution— rather than "This is the answer; there are no two ways about it." That's the sadness. We're not talking about an imagination run rampant, but rather an attempt to encourage the imagination and validate what children see. Through this digging into themselves, they really learn to become disciplined; they learn that they need to sensitize themselves, to dig deeper, and that it's work. They realize that they have a tremendous sense of freedom that they can express. They can see something, and they can have an opinion; it doesn't have to be wrong or right.

I've always had a curiosity for why things are as they are. Why does one person see something one way and another see it in a different way? And I've been curious as to how communication takes place. I've always felt that deep, deep communication could happen even though perhaps one couldn't speak. When I was younger I worked as a volunteer in Bolivia in orphanages where there were deaf and mute children. That was the beginning for me of a realization that in silence there is a language. With those children, the whole issue was silence. I began choreographing in silence, trying to find the bridge of communication. Of course, it was in the gesture and facial expression.

I've also worked with children with *given circumstances*, a phrase that I feel is the appropriate way of describing handicaps or disabilities. One episode that is especially memorable to me was a situation with a child in a wheelchair, a person no different from anyone else. When we divided into groups, she joined one group. The children were working on an image of a volcano. Given everyone's ability and disability—physical, emotional, shyness, and so forth—each child presented part of the image. The child in the wheelchair was the beginning of the volcano; she was the rumbling, the shaking—even using the wheelchair for effect. Very beautiful! She is a child, a human being, capable of communicating; it's the other children who need to understand that.

Everyone has a different way of perceiving, and everybody on this earth has a right to perceive as they choose.

* * *

Bob Blue*: It's really important for music to be fun. The songs selected for use with preschool children should be so much fun to sing that it's okay that there's a message in there. The music has to be really appealing to children. Some people do it through rock music. A lot of very young children look up to their older brothers and sisters and adopt their pace, so sometimes the music chosen will be really loud electric guitar music. It should be something that children get really excited about so that whatever message is in the song, whatever we're trying to communicate through the music, fits into the way they want to go about doing things.

They have to hear the message, though. They have to hear that the song really is making fun of something negative or is saying something important. Usually they hear the message, although sometimes it's almost as though we're putting words in their mouths, which isn't a good thing to do. But other kinds of words are put in their mouths as they're growing up, so it's nice that they hear another point of view, even if sometimes it's heavy handed.

For example, I took an issue that should be important to us, an issue that we want children to be ready for, and talked about it on their level. I wrote a song about exclusion. A girl in my class felt excluded from a friendship, and I wrote a song about it. She's White, and the two friends who are excluding her are White; but she knows what it's like to be excluded. The song is not about apartheid; it's about this little girl whose best friend deserted her and is now excluding her. It's the same message—it's unfair, it hurts—but it's right on her level. It's talking to her about what

---

Bob Blue is a second grade teacher, songwriter, and singer in Wellesley, Massachusetts. His songs have been sung by other performers around the country and the world. He has recorded one album, "Erica Levine and Friends." He is the father of three children and the stepfather of two.

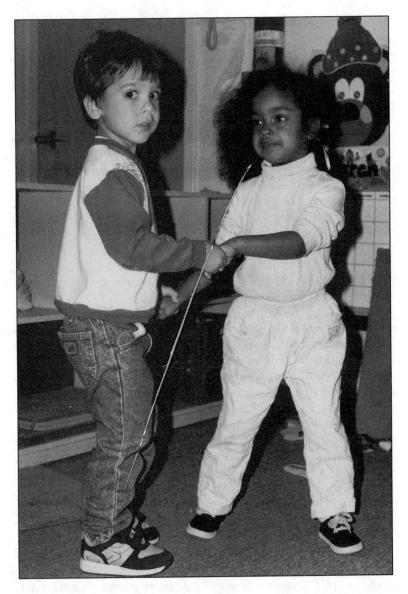

she's feeling. Later she'll grow up; and when she hears about injustice, maybe she'll think about the time that her friends excluded her.

The song needs to be simple enough and repetitive enough so that children can sing it; or, if it's not easy to learn but it's interesting enough, they'll try extra hard to learn it. It can be a tune that gets their bodies moving or sometimes just has intriguing intervals between notes. I don't concentrate too much on tunes when I write songs; I think about the words. But, in fact, the songs that seem to work for children are songs that have just the right amount of challenge in learning to sing them. Maybe it is an octave they have to sing, so their voices slide up; they love sliding their voices up to the top note they have to reach.

They also like knowing what's going to come next, however. If there are lots of verses, they like to have choruses that they can lean back on. They get really quiet during the verses because they're not sure of the words; but they know that the chorus is coming up, and they will be able to blast out the chorus. They also like learning songs in other languages because they like doing stuff that they know is hard to do and that they can do well. In the car, on the way home, they can sing a song in another language and impress their families.

One way to deal with cultural differences is to bring in music from around the world. Just the tunes from around the world give children a sense of other cultures. Learning to sing songs in other languages and what those songs mean expands their awareness of the world. Avoid songs that make only adults feel good. Some songs are ones that adults love to hear children sing because it makes adults think, "Boy, I'm really getting these kids to be idealistic." I've walked by classrooms where children are singing these songs; the children are not glowing, but the teacher is sitting there glowing. They're Mickey Mouse songs, and the children can't really sink their teeth into them.

Learning songs in other languages is one thing I do with my classes. Another is writing songs, both by myself and with children, that get them to think beyond themselves. Working with children is fun. I love singing with children; I love children's voices and their enthusiasm about singing. The reason I became a teacher and not a musician is that I wanted to make a big difference in the world. Something I learned a long time ago taught me that music is a diversion, music is not the way to make a big difference in the world. I'm not sure that's true; but so far, I feel as if teaching is the way to make a difference, and music is one of many media I use. I feel as if I'm doing something important. I'm trying to create a peaceful world, and singing with children and teaching children is my way of contributing.

*   *   *

Richard Lewis*: My work with children began with a class in literature in an art center in New Jersey. What was so exciting to me, from the first, was to reach into the imaginative lives of children and to realize the extent of their imaginations. So much of their imaginative lives seemed to be untapped and unchanneled. That moved me deeply—opening up the imagination as something integral to all human thought. That was and still is the motivating force of much of what I do—releasing and revealing to children the imagination and helping them give it shape and form.

Poetry is often a way of saying something we can't say in any other way. The beauty of all forms of art, whether poetry or painting or dance, is that art really is an alternative way of speaking about something that we find difficult to speak about using ordinary speech. And because art is often metaphoric in nature, it allows us to make our understanding of something clearer through creating the particular kind of imagery found in a poem, a story, or a dance.

With very young children I work improvisationally, making up stories and poems with them. Often these stories or poems are

Richard Lewis is an author, editor of numerous anthologies of poetry (including Miracles: Poems by Children of the English-Speaking World and In a Spring Garden), and founder and director of the Touchstone Center for Children in New York City.

based on experiences or images the children might initiate or on themes that I suggest that have universal appeal for all of us. For example, I might begin this improvisatory process by cupping my hand in such a way that it looks like a bird. As I speak about the bird who flew through the room, happy to see the sunlight again, I might ask the children to tell me what they feel like when they wake up in the morning.

As each child responds, what begins to emerge is a group—as well as an individual—expression of waking up. I might copy these verbal expressions onto a piece of paper in order to make a story or poem; or I might have each child, just as I did with the bird, show me through gesture and drama how he or she reacts to the morning. I might, if time permits, paint a large mural with the children, depicting a portrait of themselves waking up, accompanied by their verbal expressions written out on the mural itself.

Sometimes with young children I use poems from different cultures as a way of speaking about how particular persons feel about a natural phenomenon—for example, how the Eskimos feel about snow or how the Navajos feel about the dawn. The important thing is the feeling and how each of us can express a personal feeling toward anything we experience and know. The poems we read to children should act as a catalyst for their feelings and perceptions, and much of this happens when they identify not only with the imagery of the poem but with the person reading and sharing the poem as well. If the person is sensitive to the imagery within the children themselves and can help the children bring out what they are feeling, then using poetry with young children can be an inspired sharing.

My advice to teachers of young children would be to listen carefully to children as they speak with each other and with us. In their conversations children play, in effect, with so many different ideas, thoughts, and feelings. Our role is to help children use their language, their way of speaking, so that first of all, they respect it themselves. If children feel comfortable with how they express what is important to them, then their natural use of poetic and mythic language will begin to emerge. If they see that there are poems and stories by persons from cultures throughout the world that are about ideas and feelings similar to their own thinking and experiencing, then literature—not as a literary artifact, but as a living and breathing expression—will make sense to them.

SUSAN EPENETER is a consulting editor with Exchange Press, Inc.
CANDACE CHANG is the program director for Beaverbrook Guidance Center, a mental health center for children and their families in Massachusetts.

Chapter 3
STAFFING WITH DIVERSITY

"There's no substitute for personal contact with people who are 'different' to help children realize they aren't really very different at all."

—Danny Deardorff
in Seattle's Child
November 1986

Honoring Diversity: Problems and Possibilities for Staff and Organization

Margie Carter

In the early childhood field, we have many ways of referring to our work with differences: mainstreaming, multicultural, family grouping—to name a few. These terms describe our efforts to honor the needs of individual children and to recognize the pluralistic society in which we live. Many programs have chosen to specialize in one of these needs, while others try to incorporate programming for different needs into their general structure.

Most early childhood centers want their programs to represent at least a taste of living in a pluralistic society. Some centers intentionally set out to have their programs counteract our society's institutionalized discrimination based on differences, especially relating to race, culture, and sex-role biases. In each case, programs that want to accommodate differences among the children and families they serve must be clear about their goals, and they must have a responsive organizational structure.

I became acutely conscious of this when I was hired as the director of a child care program that did not have such clarity or strength in its organizational structure. It wasn't a bad program, but there was no clear vision driving it toward a set of goals or inspiring the staff or parents to come together with a sense of purpose. I found myself asking, "What if seeking, honoring, and learning from diversity became the guiding principle for all decision making and structuring of our center's program? How would our environment and curriculum look? What would change in our enrollment, finance, and personnel policies? Where would I begin making the necessary changes?"

What do we believe about diversity?

It took a period of trial and error before I realized that my first task was to create a clear philosophical statement regarding the concept of diversity. To develop a motivating vision, the staff had to come together to state what we believed and what we wanted to create. To build some common understanding and agreements about the value of diversity, we used our staff meetings to reflect on our experiences and knowledge. Over the years we deepened our insights and came to discuss them along the following lines:

• We live in a society in which differences are usually avoided, if not feared. Why is this? Often, quite unconsciously, we have absorbed concepts of *normal* and *abnormal*, *friends* and *enemies*, developed by those with the resources to shape popular culture. Through them we come to see human qualities as split into superior and inferior, righteous and evil, loser and winner. This, in turn, shapes our self-esteem, our sense of security, and our behavior when we encounter the unfamiliar.

• We tend to think in terms of the good guys and the bad guys. Psychologists tell us that the creation of enemies is often based on denied self-hatred. This notion and the understanding that our country was built on racism and attitudes such as "might makes right" and "the best and the brightest" can inform our insights into human development. Our challenge as early childhood educators is to counter these influences with a program that offers a different view and experiences from which to learn. Our goal is to develop the understanding that our security and our strength as individuals come from our interconnectedness with others. We want children to learn that all forms of life are precious and to believe that they will benefit greatly from the presence of those different from themselves.

• We know that the understanding of "strength through diversity" came long before modern economists, humanists, or civil rights advocates. In his scientific research Darwin discovered that an environment tends to be richer and more sustaining to all the life within its boundaries when many different varieties of life forms exist within that environment. What an important understanding to bring to our early childhood programs!

As we come to understand that there are truths we do not see when we use only one kind of eyes, we will seek someone different from ourselves. Conceptually, our goal of working with differences must embrace more than a strategy for civil rights or fair representation. It must include expanding our humanity and having a vision of the potential for collective growth that diversity offers.

What makes diversity work for and not against us?

Getting clear about our beliefs is an important step, but only the first of many, in honoring diversity in our early childhood programs. We need clear goals that will guide administrative policies and program and staff development. Ideal as it may seem, one program cannot include the full range of differences possible within the human family—age, sex, race, culture, religion, and physical and mental abilities. The type of differences that we incorporate into our programs must be limited to those that will enable us to remain strong and cohesive and that prevent fragmentation and divisiveness.

One of the lessons I quickly learned in my center was that although programs with diversity can be a tremendous source of strength, they are also rich in conflict. Developing guidelines for learning from our dissimilarities and creating equitable policies to address our differences are essential ingredients for making the whole idea work.

What personnel policies strengthen diversity?

If diversity is a program priority, it will immediately be visible among the staff. This is our greatest challenge, given today's staff shortages and poverty-level wages. It is a formidable task to not only find but *keep* desirable teachers. When a diverse group of people come together to consciously influence the next generation, the personal and professional growth available to them is enormous. To a certain extent this opportunity can offset the negative aspects of the salary and stress. The task then is to translate this motivational factor into an effective staff recruitment program. A polished marketing package may help in this effort, but the primary recruitment will come from those staff members who enthusiastically and regularly tell others outside the program about their work and growth.

Recruitment. A program that serves multiethnic families is usually conscientious in seeking a diverse staff to provide role models for the children. If the program population is primarily homogeneous, it is even more important that we diversify our staff so as not to further a misrepresentation of the world in our learning environments. Staff hiring can be approached with an informal needs assessment or a rigorous affirmative action plan.

Gentle Dragon Child Care Center in Seattle, Washington, has chosen the latter approach. For their overall program their policy is to have a staff that is 60% non-White and 40% White. Within each classroom the center strives for a staff balance of at least one male, one Spanish-speaking person, and one person who knows sign

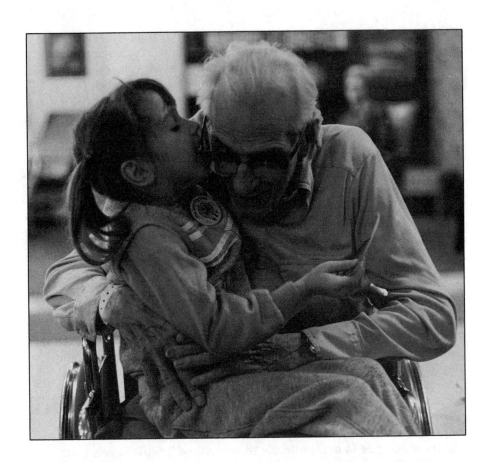

language. Through the Foster Grandparent Program, they also ensure that there is a grandparent for each class. To parallel their enrollment policies, Gentle Dragon also seeks to have at least 20% of their staff represent alternative family structures.

Following similar guidelines, Thorndike Street School in Cambridge, Massachusetts, has developed a plan they call "affirmative outreach." When a staff vacancy occurs they send a job description and flyer announcing the opening to community agencies that represent the diverse populations they seek. The mailing is followed by phone calls. If necessary, they place ads on radio stations and in publications that target these populations.

Employment criteria. When hiring staff I have discovered that I bring unconscious assumptions about age, economic circumstances, family, or cultural backgrounds to interview arrangements and questions. If I haven't thought through how these factors influence a candidate, I may unintentionally discriminate against the very person who would be an asset to the program. Is English literacy a high priority for this staff position? If not, the written application shouldn't be given too much weight. Am I seeking a grandparent figure to complement my staff? My interview questions then need to focus on the experiences of the candidate, rather than her or his career path—"What has been most difficult for you in being with three-year-olds?" rather than "What do you hope to be doing five years from now?" If I am open to hiring or am seeking a single parent for the staff, I shouldn't schedule the interview at a time that complicates child care arrangements. When people with physical or mental disabilities are to be included on the staff, interviewing arrangements must be suited to those circumstances.

Personnel policies. Personnel policies that address differing life circumstances will serve to attract a diverse staff. There is a delicate balance to be struck between the needs of the program and the group as a whole and those of the individuals. Again, the policies of the Gentle Dragon and Thorndike Street programs can provide helpful examples.

Gentle Dragon Child Care established its program as a worker-owned and -managed collective. Recognizing that education, training, and experience are often the result of race, gender, and economic privilege in our unjust society, they decided to make the base pay for all staff equal. Additional salary, benefits, and all work arrangements are then offered according to need, rather than according to qualifications of education, experience, or seniority. Wage increments are offered for dependent children or parents. A health allowance is available for those whose health care needs cannot be met through traditional insurance policies. Parental leave is available for women and men, including adoptive parents. Child care fees are reduced to one-third for staff members. Floating paid holidays have been included to allow for religious and cultural differences. In-service training for staff members includes management skills training—a tremendous opportunity for those who might never have envisioned this for themselves.

The Thorndike Street School began offering an equal hourly wage for all, but they discovered that as staff gained experience and training, they moved on to higher paying jobs for which they were then qualified. In an effort to retain their staff, they changed the salary structure to include entry level and seniority wage differences and established assistant teacher positions for new teachers. This enabled their program to offer job mobility and a training base for those entering the early childhood education field for the first time or those moving from family day care homes to child care centers. The creativity that both of these programs have brought to their personnel policies has made them attractive to diverse populations.

How do we build cohesiveness in the midst of diversity?

As diversity on a staff increases, so do the possible problem areas. Continual work must be done to build group consensus and team spirit. We must take care not to assume that everyone sees things in the same way, and we must take time to discover, appreciate, and learn from our differences. In doing so, we will recognize that both family backgrounds and cultural beliefs and practices influence the assumptions and behaviors we have acquired.

In her book, *Teaching Adults: An Active Learning Approach,* Elizabeth Jones discusses methods she has used to help teachers become aware of what influences their own development, in order to better understand their work in the child development field. She asks people to look over a list of characteristics used to describe an *ideal child.* First they are to check the characteristics that indicate the kind of person their parents wanted them to become and to cross off those characteristics considered undesirable and usually discouraged or punished. They then repeat the process, indicating the kind of person they would like their child to become. This exercise provokes passionate discussion and deeper insights into oneself and one's co-workers.

On other occasions Jones has concluded a brief lecture introducing the concept of culture by asking those in the group who can confidently name their culture to stand up and do so. The rest of the group then joins those standing, forming small cluster groups to identify the different beliefs and behaviors of each culture named. This exercise helps teachers to distinguish fact from fiction in cultural stereotypes and also to uncover the discrepancies that occur between beliefs and behaviors. Incorporating such activities into our staff meetings will help us get to know ourselves and each other better. We may also clarify changes we want to make to overcome any acquired biases or behaviors that we don't want to pass along to the children in our care.

Regular staff meetings are essential for communication and decision making in diverse groups. Without them, routine concerns can become a major source of tension. I remember well a center discussion on whether to have a policy requiring the children to eat all of their food before leaving the table. One teacher said, "My family always used the line about the poor, starving Chinese, and I hated it." Another added, "We were never forced to eat anything in my family, and I think that has limited my acquired tastes." Almost under her breath a third voice said, "We just hoped there was enough food on the table when I was growing up." Almost by accident this staff discussion uncovered these dramatically different experiences influencing our views. It deepened our understanding and appreciation of each other and caused us to draw closer together as a staff. From there we were able to more objectively discuss what message we wanted to convey to the children and to set our policy accordingly.

On another occasion the staff took up the question of what the center should do for Halloween. One teacher explained that the more she was reading about the historic role of witches as midwives, healers, and mediators in primitive cultures, the more uncomfortable she felt with the Halloween stereotype of witches as wicked and evil. "It's like blaming the victim. These women were burned at the stake by the thousands for their beliefs and practices." Another teacher spoke up, "In my church we are told not to celebrate Halloween because it is a pagan practice based on demons and sin. I've always hated it for that reason." Because the goal of the discussion was to explore and understand, the thinking of each of us was broadened by hearing these differing views. We created a Halloween party that centered around the lesson that it is not only fun but instructive to pretend to be someone you really aren't—learning what life is like behind that mask.

Each of these examples could have been occasions for staff conflicts, divisions, and tensions, but instead we used them to bring us closer together across our differences. This happened not only because of the value we placed on diversity but because of the concrete way we provided for staff discussions, using active listening and problem-solving practices.

Things, of course, do not always go this smoothly. With the demands and stresses of child care work, staff tensions can mount to an intense level. To prevent things from deteriorating into personality conflicts or duplicities, we need a reference point against which we can test our assumptions and standards regarding acceptable staff behaviors. Such standards, along with a statement of how conflicts will be handled, should be included in written personnel policies, if not staff contracts.

Ideally, these expectations and approaches to conflict resolution will parallel what we have set out for the children in our program. For instance, a statement might read, "At our center we all share in caring for each other and for the environment. When someone forgets or breaks this agreement, we remind them of how it hurts the group, explore why this happened, and work together to help the person get back on track. We work out disagreements by taking turns listening carefully to each other, explaining what we understand, and exploring what changes are possible and acceptable to those involved."

Over the years our staff developed a paper called "Staff Agreements and Approaches to Criticism When Agreements Are Broken" (see box on pp. 78–79). These agreements proved invaluable in helping us prevent unproductive criticisms based on subjective opinions or preferences. The investigative aspect countered the human tendency to become judgmental or defensive during a conflict.

What do our programs teach children about diversity?

Adult modeling accounts for a good part of what is significant for the children in our programs. The effectiveness of the environments we create for them, the materials we provide, and the curriculum we design are dependent on our interactions with the children and with each other.

Staff Agreements and Approaches to Criticism When Agreements Are Broken

1. We will each have an attitude of flexibility and cooperation in our work here, thinking of the needs of others and the group as a whole, along with our own needs.

2. We will each carry a full share of the workload, which includes some extra hours outside our work schedule (i.e., parent-teacher conferences, meetings, planning and preparation of activities, recordkeeping, progress reports).

3. We will each communicate directly and honestly with each other. We will be respectful and honorable in our interactions.

4. When problems or difficulties related to our work arise, we will address them rather than ignore or avoid them.

5. We will all be informed of significant problems that affect the center. These will be communicated in person as soon as possible and in writing as necessary.

6. We understand that it is appropriate to seek help from the director on sensitive or difficult issues.

7. When necessary, we will use a criticism/self-criticism discussion process to identify attitudes and behaviors that are negatively affecting our agreements.

Criticism/Self-Criticism Process

to investigate and educate so we continue to adhere to our agreements

Much has been written about the importance of a multicultural curriculum in early childhood programs. What is important to emphasize here is that our curriculum approaches should indicate that there are many ways of seeing and living in the world, rather than conveying the message that the White Western view is *normal* and these others are exotic, supplemental, and different, but not normal.

This means that rather than teaching a special lesson about Japan, we should include chopsticks, bowls, Japanese food packages, kimonos, tatami mats, and pagodas in our housekeeping areas, or units about food, clothing, and shelter. Pictures around the room, fabrics, dolls, puzzles, and other learning materials

Questions to ask oneself before giving a criticism:

1. Is my criticism based on investigation or on assumption?

2. What is the most important element of the criticism? Secondary?

3. What is my side of the problem, my responsibility, or my contribution to it?

4. What are my disguises that keep me from being criticized?

5. Is my criticism intended to hurt or attack, or is it to educate?

6. How are our agreements hurt or helped by what I am criticizing?

7. How can I play a concrete, positive role in helping the other person change?

8. What changes do I need to make in myself?

Stating a criticism:

When you do . . .

I feel . . .

It hurts our agreements because . . .

Therefore I want you to . . .

In the future I will behave differently by . . .

Investigative discussion of the criticism:

Why do you feel that way? What happened?

What other things were going on? (objective things happening; subjective impressions, feelings)

What is the main thing that needed to happen here?

should reflect diversity. When we teach about transportation, we can include methods of transport that are used in a variety of cultures.

This approach is especially important for programs with a fairly homogeneous population. Children often respond to the unfamiliar with fear or rejection. Our task is to help them see differences as normal, familiar, acceptable, and useful.

The language we use is a crucial factor in how children come to view differences. Although we want to teach them names for things, we want to avoid labels that reinforce stereotypes that the predominant culture is conveying. Labels often confine understandings and thus acceptance. It is good to first describe what is being referred to before labeling it. "Taiko's eyes are brown, and they are

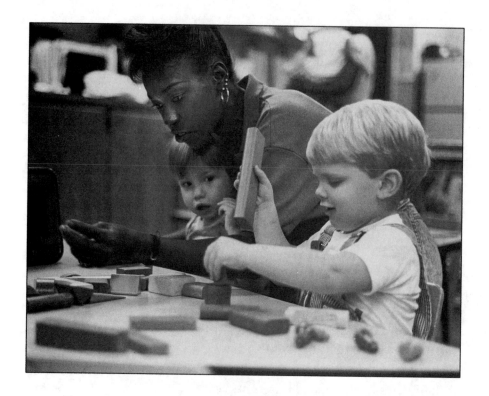

shaped like this. That's one of the ways you can know she comes from an Asian culture" or "Jack's ears have trouble hearing. We call that being deaf." We don't want to convey that there is something wrong with a child who is the only one with certain characteristics. This not only isolates and defeats self-esteem for the child who is different, but it creates the impression for the other children that their characteristics are more acceptable.

References to families is another area where we must take care with our assumptions and language. Before the current prevalence of single-parent families, many teachers automatically referred to families as mommy and daddy. We now recognize how that isolates the child who lives with only one parent and how it conveys the sense that this is not normal.

Less statistically visible, there are children in our program who are being parented by a grandparent or aunt, or who live with foster parents, gay parents, or a large extended family with many persons taking a parenting role. Our discussions of family life need to convey plurality and inclusiveness rather than pity, shame, or shock. Explorative discussions in staff meetings can enhance thinking and planning for the differences that exist in family structures and circumstances.

Does diversity come first in our enrollment practices?

Both Gentle Dragon and the Thorndike Street School make *intake choices* from the children on their waiting lists. Because of their commitment to diversity, they follow many of the same *affirmative outreach* approaches to enrollment that are used with staff recruitment. Quotas are set for certain populations, and spaces are reserved for them. Fees are determined in a similar manner, allowing for a variety of economic circumstances. All of this can be quite tedious at times, if not financially risky. "Sometimes we get quite scared that we won't make our budget," exclaims a Gentle Dragon collective member. "But if we hold firm, the rewards are really worth it. One of our primary goals is to offer a multicultural learning experience to children of a variety of backgrounds and beliefs; thus, cultural diversity is our highest priority in enrollment."

Where will it all lead?

Certain ideas and experiences have the power to transform our lives. If learning and growing from differences is a goal for the adults, and if they have an organizational structure responsive to that goal, the goal will be achieved for the children as well. Who knows where this might all lead? Perhaps it will be powerful enough to help in the transformation of our country as a whole. I'm a believer. Are you?

Reference

Jones, E. (1986). *Teaching adults: An active learning approach.* Washington, DC: NAEYC.

MARGIE CARTER is an early childhood instructor for Pacific Oaks College and several Seattle area community colleges. She is a consultant for Head Start centers and child care programs in the state of Washington and is a member of the Anti-bias Leadership Project. Margie's contribution to this book is written in memory of Lenora Banks, a child care teacher who contributed greatly to Margie's commitment to diversity in early childhood programs.

Are You a Dad AND a Teacher? Fathering—A Year-Long Curriculum

Cory Gann and Sharon Stine

As an administrator, I greeted a request by one of my teachers to bring a baby to work with a mixture of anticipation and doubt. I had had previous experiences that raised questions and concerns about the difficulties of being both teacher and parent in a program for young children, but I was excited about the new kinds of learning this situation would offer to preschool children. Because Cory, the teacher making this request, was a father, I felt that this was a special opportunity for children to experience on a day-to-day basis their teacher as a nurturing daddy. Perhaps this would have an impact on young children's understandings of what men do. To implement a curriculum that was a natural interweaving of children's understandings of gender roles seemed worth the risk.

We began with careful planning, trying to predict what Cory's day might be like. Complexity was a major issue. We thrive when there is a healthy match between the complexity of our work and our ability to cope. When there isn't enough complexity, we get bored and search for something to add spice. When there is too much complexity, we get overwhelmed. And the need for complexity varies with the individual. Basically, I wanted to lessen the complexity for Cory, knowing that Caitlin, his 10-month-old, would be adding enough complexity! We decided that teaching half time would be a realistic teaching load.

Staff support was essential, so our second task was to develop clear descriptions of what Cory would do and what might be difficult for him. This was discussed with team teachers and finally written down as specific job descriptions to clarify the situation for everyone.

Two issues emerged for Cory. First, how would he feel in a setting where he was supposed to know how to raise children but would be constantly on view to staff, students, and parents? Second, would he be able to stick to the more limited job description (half time) and not be seduced into overextending himself? What follows is Cory's story, which describes his weaving a texture of fathering into the daily lives of 40 children, three and four years old, during a year together in a morning preschool program.

Get set . . . go

FLASHBACK. It's 7:53, and Caitlin and I are on our mark, get set, go for *seat wars*. She braces, then arches her back with more strength than I imagined from a 10-month-old baby. Megan, her six-year-old sister, complains that her seat belt is wedged. This morning's buckling is complicated by Caitlin's bulky coat. She gets lost in it, and the buckles don't fit over the fiberfill. I finish a quick inventory: Megan's lunch box, Caitlin's diaper carrier, plastic bag, backpack, bottle, extra juice, blanket for Caitlin, my coffee, and materials for an art project. Yes, I am actually teaching today! We

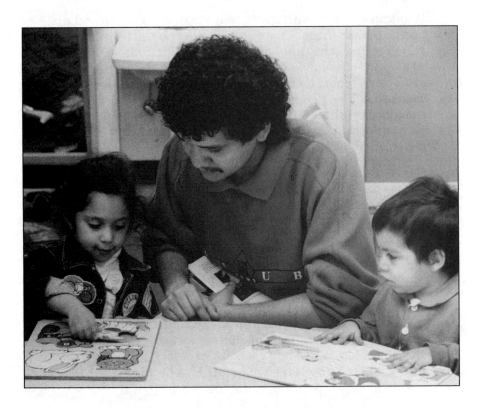

roll out of the driveway, hot on the heels of the bottleneck traffic jam lined up at the freeway on-ramp.

Inching along, I reflect on what's going on: In 40 households scattered around the city, parents and their children are scampering around, putting their own unique finishing touches on post-breakfast rituals designed to get them up and out, moving in tandem toward one common destination—to deliver their pre-schoolers to the Pacific Oaks play yard to be nurtured by a group of trained educators that includes me. Megan's first grade teacher, Ms. Knudsen, is busily setting up the science center that Megan will explore once Caitlin and I deliver her to the gate of her class-room. Then we will hightail it back to the freeway to get to our destination and get ready for those 40 preschoolers. So, as I see it, 40 families are beating their brains out to get to me, while I'm beating my brains out to get Megan to Ms. Knudsen; and Caitlin is scrunched in her car seat ready to embark on a day of nurturing by her part-time teacher, full-time daddy. Now that I've got that straight, I'm ready for the day.

Settling in

Caitlin and I arrived surreptitiously, easing up the preschool stairs at a toddler's rate. Our entrance was characterized often by Caitlin's guarded gaze that said, "I think I'll just make myself invisible today!" Sensitive co-teachers neither chorused nor ignored our arrival but greeted us naturally, as if nothing out of the ordinary was happening. This daddy with his baby was ready, so he thought, to serve the needs of these three- and four-year-olds as well.

I was instantly impressed by the natural groupings. We settled on the periphery of an activity, and there they were, like mercury from a smashed thermometer regathering itself into a ball: Evan, Jessica, Marshall, Jonathan, Megan, Lucera—each told their daily story of what their baby brother or sister does at home, or how they cried when they were 10 months old, or some expostulation about the general nature of raising babies. "It's hard!" said Jessica. "My mom works all the time." Here was a discussion, a conversa-tion (language arts), each child in his or her own turn, listening to me and the others. Here was a self-selected group, organically cast, convening (at least for a while on a daily basis), anticipating the morning's coming together. Most surprising to me was the self-generating nature of it, inspired at first by Caitlin's presence, but then taking on a life of its own. The children were clearly here because they liked the conversation. We had colloquium of four-year-olds going, and once in a while we (yes, even I) got annoyed at Caitlin's fussiness.

The programmed baby unit we tried as an extension of our official family group structure went much differently. Caitlin and I regularly visited each small group of children at 11:30. I did baby care. We ate together—this group of preschoolers, teachers, and a 10-month-old—and then I changed the baby. Children would get turns holding pins and diapers, watching and commenting, initiating discussions of anatomy and sex roles. *What Is a Girl? What Is a Boy?*, a marvelous children's book, was propped ready on the bookcase; anatomically correct dolls were available for immediate dramatic play. The lesson we learned from all of this preparation and planning derived, not from Caitlin or the other children, but rather from the set of attribute blocks with which most of the children busied themselves once eating was finished and Caitlin had inconsiderately nodded off. "Aha," I commented professorially to my teaching assistant. "One of the essential attributes of attribute blocks is that they don't take morning naps."

Where is her mom?

I must confess to having the same thought a time or two myself when the whole of it just got to me. But important questions come in spurts and bits, the tender topic talk and the tenderly rigid views of preoperational thinkers. "Is it a boy or a girl?" Evan asked daily, only the syntax of the question changing from time to time. "Is THAT baby a boy or a girl?" Evan greeted us one particular morning and I couldn't help correlating his emphatic tone with Caitlin's attire for the day—blue coveralls and a sweatshirt complemented by her standard you-go-anywhere-you-want baby hairstyle. "Where's her mom?" was Catherine's query, echoed several times a week by classmates trying to get used to the two of us.

When Caitlin fell or scraped herself, "Where's her mom?" got my more curt response. "At work!" I would say, holding Caitlin while she cried, hugged me tightly, and lapsed into recuperative quiet. As her playfulness returned, I conversed more freely with a few still-concerned companions. "Her mother is a teacher just like me, only at a different school with older children. So I take care of Caitlin during the day." We all walked inside to change Caitlin's diaper. The children held pins and set down the changing pad. Caitlin kicked her legs to make a better test of my competency with an audience. Task completed, Caitlin rolled herself into a crawling position just in time for Evan to ask once again, "Is your baby a boy or a girl?" I'm left to wonder about the preschooler's conservation of gender, at least when it comes to babies.

But sometimes I wonder

Caitlin's fussiness threshold was three minutes at the sandbox and four-and-a-half minutes in the trike area. It did not occur to me that by bringing my baby with me to work I was also embarking on a regime of what could be called *teaching in motion* or, as one metaphorically inclined co-worker observed, "teaching as if you have to go to the bathroom all the time." Wonderful teaching moments were balanced by the limitations of my own baby's unpredictable demands, when I had to move on. At the same time, one of the effects Caitlin had on me was to cause me to constantly think of her needs rather than the needs I had as a teacher. Leaving the sandbox or trike path so precipitously could also be described as your basic *leaving children in the lurch*. The antidote for me was a clear yell for help to other staff as we bounced our way out of the sandbox on to the next step of "roving and floating," as it's known in the lexicon.

Caitlin's presence did have an effect on both the children and myself as we dealt with social problems. On more than one occasion, Caitlin stood squarely between two momentary combatants, trustfully calibrating the escalation of emotion: "I had it first!" "No, I did!" "No, I did!"

Even amid hotly agitated disputes, our three- and four-year-olds tempered their ferocity in deference to Caitlin's petite innocence. Maybe she lent a measure of perspective to all of those ego-tinged conflicts. The truth of the matter is that she emerged unscathed from one fray after another.

I did plunge in less often than I would have if Caitlin hadn't been there, which worked to the behavioral objective of *letting kids work it out for themselves*. But I sometimes wonder! What do children lose when we don't take that teacher step that has all the earmarks of *just the right move*? I remember a fairly complex play drama that was unfolding one morning in front of the climbing structure. London and Geoffrey were driving the large rectangular box, bedecked in yellow raincoats and firefighter hats, obviously immersed in a fire-engine scenario. What impressed me was the careful inclusion of useful and symbolic things that were fetched deliberately within a matter of minutes. London brought over one of the smaller ladders and hooked it along the side of the box. Geoffrey propped a sandbox shovel into the crate's handle groove, creating a convenient post for the coiled fire hose (15-foot jump rope). Even an adult could envision this hook-and-ladder, siren blasting its way through the rush-hour congestion of the preschool yard.

Sergio deftly attempted to become part of this game by sidestepping the normal social steps of entreaty and negotiation, assuming

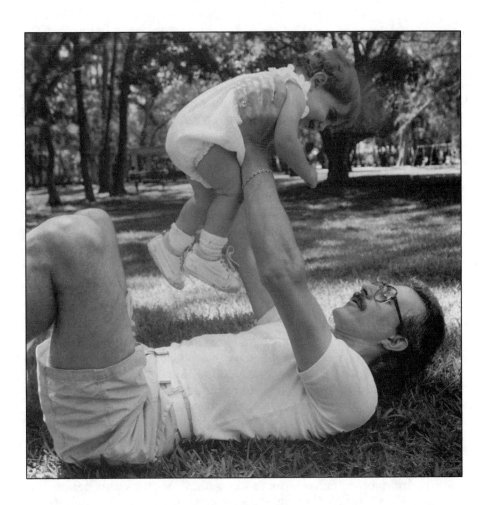

instead the cadence of this scene. He yelled "Fire!" at the top of his lungs and pointed to the upper deck of the climbing structure. Geoffrey quickly unraveled the rope/hose and leapt up in hot pursuit of the "burning embers."

The teacher voice within me chimed in loudly about what my next move ought to be. *"Move that green garden hose sitting near the ramp closer to their truck. Be unassuming, and you don't need to say a word. See if the addition of the real hose anchors their play and facilitates the inclusion of Sergio."* The clarity of this message charged my nerve endings and practically mobilized the rest of me into action, only to ram full force into the gentle daddy of me sitting patiently on the porch steps, nestling my baby in my lap! The two of us were sharing the story unfolding before our eyes.

In a moment Geoffrey and London were off and away. Sergio was left lamenting the refrain, "They won't play with me . . . ."

What did you learn, Cory?

Just before the end of the school year, Megan asked if she could skip one day of first grade in order to spend the morning with Caitlin and me. We chose the day, and Megan selected a favorite picture book to read to the four-year-olds during their group time. The influence of a six-year-old story reader held the children spellbound for several pages. Gradually, the listeners drifted away to work on their end-of-the-year remembrance albums of photos and art work. As three or four children got started on the project, Megan forged ahead in her book with the remaining story hold-outs. Caitlin veritably pranced in a circle, pulling selective papers off the shelves and humming a made-up tune to herself as she had started to do those days.

As the memory books took form and shape, each child commenced the task of signing the cover page, each with his or her degree of legibility and competence, some already adding flourishing strokes, some omitting the tougher letters. Marshall offered an editorial comment in the middle of writing his name: "S is the difficult letter. I always used to mess it up." I responded, "It's amazing, Marshall. In September you couldn't write any letters, and now here you are signing your name. And at the start of school, Megan didn't know how to read, and now here she is reading a story to the whole group. And not only did Caitlin learn how to walk, she is dancing around!" Lily dotted her *i* and admired her work for a second; then she asked, "What did you learn, Cory?"

To answer Lily's question, I didn't really learn something *new* as much as I learned it *better*. In a way, Caitlin became everyone's sibling during the ten months, adding all of the joys and headaches the arrival of a new baby sister brings. I remember being prone to an unusual cringe when loving children in my class would, uninvited, pick Caitlin up from behind, only to be on the receiving end of a well-decibeled squelch she had developed for such occasions. Caitlin was a catalyst for the emerging sense of *other* which it is every preschooler's task to develop—another person, even so small, with other feelings, responses, expectations, and, of course, rights.

As a parent at work, the *other directedness* of Caitlin's presence was a humbling experience. With Caitlin I was having to think all the time about behaviors that caused me not to be a *good* teacher in the eyes of others. Here was somebody I cared about on a minute-to-minute basis even more than my job performance! A song not finished, an art activity never quite set up, the answer to a question trailed in the wake of my baby's more immediate need— these are recollections to chuckle about with Caitlin when one day we thumb through snapshots of our year together. For my class, I hope that these will not matter at all, or hardly as much as the experiencing of their teacher—a father—and his baby.

Weaving it all together

Bringing a baby to work is an individual decision, but it impinges on many people who become the network of caring, understanding, and support. By trying something that none of us had done before, we knew that the risk carried unknowns that would trip us up from time to time. When tensions resulted—"Cory is always holding that

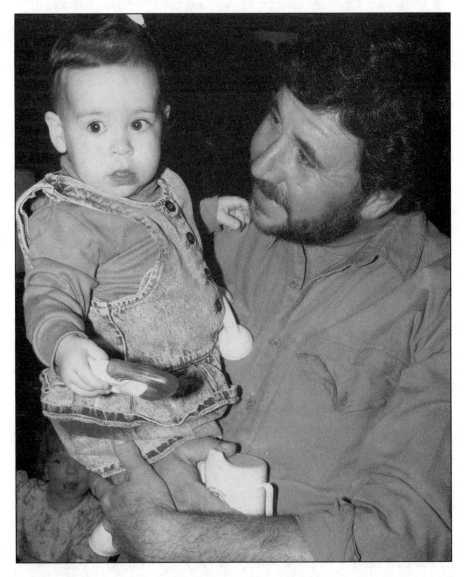

baby!"—*staff talked out their frustrations. Babies make different demands; their needs must often come first. Not only was the teaching team working with this issue, the children were also learning when their teacher was needed by his baby. They became more aware of their teacher as a family member. He didn't live at school; he had a baby and a home with the baby's mother and sister. Their comments about families, particularly their own, were a window to a growing interest in figuring out about mothers, fathers, siblings, babies, and, ultimately, their place in these linkings of people.*

Although teachers bucked up against new frustrations, one of the known factors that added stability to the program was that the staff had worked together before. They already had established a teaching relationship that included a willingness to talk about problems immediately, to share feelings, frustrations, and some delightful humor and playfulness.

Our early assessments of what Cory would be able to do and what would be difficult for him were very close to the mark. That initial thinking, writing, and clarifying of everyone's roles formed a foundation of needed predictions. Before our daily experiences began, we had discussed the difficult reality that Cory might have to pull out if the program was not working for Caitlin (the plan's most unpredictable ingredient). Even though this didn't happen, looking at the issue early in our planning stages gave everyone a better understanding of some limits of this unknown venture.

Our story is not necessarily a model for other programs. Rather, it points out the need to develop curriculum about sex differences that includes daily experiences with fathering models—experiences that are ongoing rather than occasional appendages. When we limit ourselves to a theme plan, such as a week of gender-role activities, we run the risk of providing an exotic tourist curriculum in which being a nurturing male is the unusual, not the day-to-day way people live as loving human beings.

Reference

Waxman, S. (1976). *What Is a Girl? What Is a Boy?* Culver City, CA: Peace Press.

CORY GANN teaches seven- and eight-year-old children at The Little School in Bellevue, Washington. He is active in promoting an antibias perspective in education, which was the topic of his dissertation at Claremont College Graduate School in California.

SHARON STINE is a professor in the Department of Environmental Studies at the California State Polytechnic University, Pamona. She teaches human factor issues—particularly those related to children, culture, age, accessibility, and gender—to landscape architects, architects, and urban planners. From 1980 to 1986 she was dean of children's programs at Pacific Oaks College.

Chapter 4
LEARNING FROM PARENTS

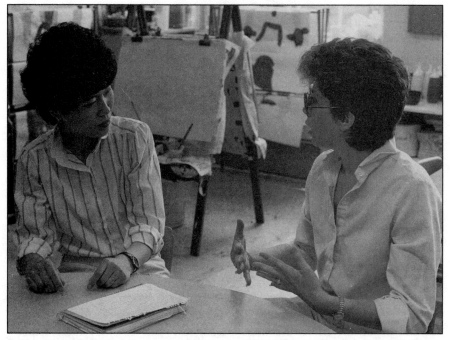

"For adults, consciousness raising is often needed to move from a state of ignoring differences to one of identifying and joyfully exploring differences."

—Mary Lynn Porter
Auburn Day Care Centers
Auburn, Alabama

Tossed Salad Is Terrific: Values of Multicultural Programs for Children and Families

Janet Brown McCracken

"Mom," four-year-old Erica asked as we climbed into the car to start the commute home, "are we juice?"

"Are we juice?" I repeated in a puzzled voice.

"Yes, are we juice?" she insisted. "All the juice kids pretended to be Moses and the people who got treated mean, but I had to watch."

It was then that I recalled seeing a notice that a parent was going to make potato latkes with the children in Erica's child care center for Seder, as part of Passover. Erica wanted to be Jewish, too, so she could be a part of the action!

All through Erica's five-and-a-half years in the Broadcasters' Child Development Center in Washington, D.C., we have had the privilege of knowing a variety of parents and teachers, in a supportive setting, who wanted the best for children—some are middle-income White, like us; many others are Black, Asian, and Spanish-speaking. The experiences all of us have shared and the warm feelings about the potpourri of people we have come to admire, respect, and love will last a lifetime. This wealth of opportunities could never really be duplicated by a family without the advantages of a high-quality child care program that instills in staff and families alike the value of individuals—a tossed salad approach, rather than a melting pot in which everyone is expected to conform to one set of expectations.

Knowing real people

The good feelings about the value of this type of multicultural education are built around the small, everyday incidents in which children, parents, and teachers come to know each other as people. These experiences are far from trivial because they are the reality of everyday life, shared with others. No artificial celebrations of holidays; books or movies about other people; visits to museums; or any other secondary experiences could possibly have the impact that these valued human relationships—with parents, teachers, and children—have had in cementing a genuine respect for people. Let's look together at how such everyday contact with others forms the basis of a strong multicultural program for families.

Teresa Reyes, a teacher of toddlers, immigrated from Bolivia and has just become a U.S. citizen. She often speaks to the children in Spanish, so much of their first language has a Spanish inflection, and the early exposure to Spanish still appears occasionally in their speech. The value of this early exposure to the variety of language was evident on our family vacation in Canada when Erica was four years old. She quickly picked up the rhythm of the French she encountered and delighted in playing waitress—in French. Erica still says "lellow" instead of "yellow" and adamantly denies that she speaks English. It may well be that this interest in languages, and the ability to hear and repeat various inflections, will serve these children well the rest of their lives.

Teresa's niece, Gigi, and Erica became best friends as toddlers. Four years later they continue to greet each other with hugs and talk about each other frequently, although they rarely get together. The depth of the girls' friendship was demonstrated when Gigi's mother was about to remarry; Gigi was resistant to the idea. Erica has been through a similar situation, so Teresa asked Erica if she could talk with Gigi about it. Erica enthusiastically told Gigi, "I was a grown-up flower girl at Mom and Jim's wedding. And you know what? It's great to have two dads. Some people have two moms and some have two dads." Erica's support clearly helped Gigi feel more comfortable in dealing with her blended family.

Birthdays are another important time for families from different cultures to share. Erica has attended two of Gigi's birthday parties where she was one of the few English-speaking children. "We had a great time, Mom. When can I go back to Gigi's again to play with her and her friends? Her new dad was real nice, too."

Teresa's generosity, even on her abysmally inadequate teacher's salary, has led her to insist on making Erica's birthday cake for her party at school. The low-sugar cake, her mother's specialty, is always beautifully decorated with the symbols most meaningful

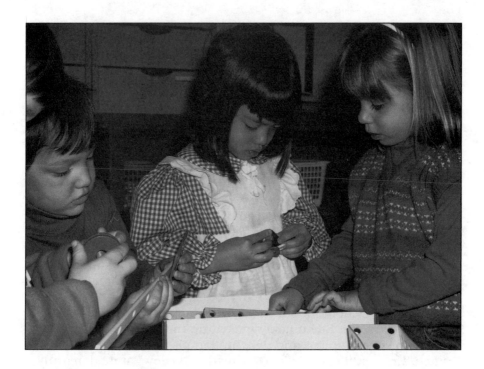

to Erica—for her fifth birthday the cake was graced with a beautiful rainbow.

Teresa's cheerful greetings every morning and her genuine interest in every family in the center have added immeasurably to the love and valuing of the diversity of wonderful people.

Another long-time staff member, Shirley Watkins, teaches the oldest group, and parents are always so pleased when their children finally reach Shirley's team—they have seen how wonderful she is! Shirley has that rare gift of natural respect for people of all ages. She exudes warmth and understanding, whether the parent or the child is having a difficult time. As a Black parent with four children, she knows what to expect even in the most difficult situations, and she knows just how to listen and respond with soothing and comforting words.

The "Shirley stories" she tells about her own childhood clearly hold the children spellbound because the children can relate so well to her experiences. One powerful story that is a favorite of the children (complete with appropriate gestures and sound effects) follows:

One night Shirley took a bath (washing motions). *She went upstairs and her Grandmother tucked* (tucking the covers in) *her into bed. She tricked her Grandmother into thinking that she was asleep. Shirley tiptoed downstairs* (finger to the lips and spoken quietly) *and then opened the door. And then she played in her sandbox. And then her Grandmother went downstairs and locked the door because she didn't know Shirley wasn't in her bed. Then Shirley heard scratching noises* (fingers scraping faster and faster). (With much animation)*They got louder and louder and she was scared! She tried to get back into the house, but the door was locked and she couldn't get in. She knocked on the door* (knocking) *and her Grandmother let her in. When her Grandmother picked her up* (hugging), *Shirley peed all over and said to herself she would never do that again! Then she took another bath and then she went to bed.*

Shirley's ability to help children figure out solutions to their own problems is unparalleled. She demonstrates caring and respect when she listens. Parents and children alike learn a great deal about how to relate to people from Shirley.

There are many other people and experiences in a multicultural center such as Broadcasters' Child Development Center that are memorable. Bob, for instance, who was first a teacher of toddlers and then a preschool teacher, speaks not only English but also Spanish and Chinese. He was delighted when two Chinese children, Paul and Stephanie, enrolled at the center. During those years every child in their groups frequently found her or his name (or symbol) written in Chinese. Erica still loves Chinese food, thanks to the cooking experiences at the center and her close friendships with Paul and Stephanie.

Bob left the center in the summer of 1985 to serve as a volunteer in war-torn Nicaragua before beginning graduate work in bilingual education. There were many anxious moments for parents, teachers, and children alike while he was gone. While driving to the center each day, we heard the news. Every time Nicaragua was mentioned, which was frequently, Erica (and I) would get a worried look on her face and note anxiously, "That's where Bob is!" His letters assured all of us that his work with children there was going well; but more than a year after his return, the word *Nicaragua* still elicits an amazed, "That's where Bob went!"

One child in the program, Liana, was adopted at the age of three from Korea, where life had been excruciatingly difficult for her. She spoke no English, but all of the children immediately welcomed her and made her feel at home. Bob and Shirley did, too, of course, and it was their special understanding that helped Liana pick up English and friends faster than it seemed possible. This energy-filled, outgoing child soon became a big sister and left the program. That was nearly two years ago. Erica still talks about seeing Liana arrive at the public school upstairs with her baby sister. Never once has she mentioned the fact that Liana has a large birthmark on her face—to her, Liana is one of many close friends.

There are many other families and children whom we have come to know and love. Marge Kumaki's patience, with a four-year-old and a new infant, is exceptional. Many of us admire her ability to be so calm as she arrives every morning with diapers, lunches, clothes, and bottles in hand. And yet she often reads a story with a small group of attentive children at the end of a hectic day at work! Or Reggie Todd, the father who so skillfully held his newborn son throughout the preschool parents' meeting for his older daughter. By observing other parents and teachers, all of us can learn so much from each other about what it takes to make the world a great place for children.

Work times are yet another example of how the diverse skills and needs of parents and staff can be recognized and met. Together, families from various backgrounds serve as board members, work on fundraisers, and find ways to achieve our common goal: the best possible experiences for young children from three months old to five years old in a full-day program.

Without the context of a multicultural center, none of us would ever have had the opportunity to feel so close to such a variety of interesting people. Our children have grown up, from infancy, surrounded by people who are proud of their ethnicity, and at

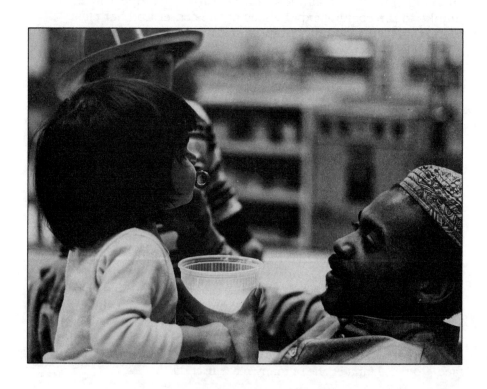

times each child has expressed a desire to be what the other children are. This is healthy because they have not learned to stereotype people based on a preconceived notion of them. The children and families know—and admire—each other because they know and respect each other.

It was not until Erica was four years old that she gave any indication that she noticed skin color, and then only in passing she inquired whether someone "was Black like Anthony." She has always accepted people just as they are; and with such a firm foundation, she and her friends always will.

The future

The tossed salad approach to early childhood education has been a marvelous complement to the lives of every person in the program. Many of the families have talked about how we anticipate that these rich opportunities will continue as our children enter elementary schools. We all hope that there are other cultures in these new settings that will enable us to broaden our world view even further.

JANET BROWN MCCRACKEN, M.Ed., is an early childhood education consultant with Subjects & Predicates and is a former director of publications for the National Association for the Education of Young Children. She is a mother of two children.

Building Positive Images: Interracial Children and Their Families

Francis Wardle

"Teacher, who's that lady?"

"Which lady, Johnny?"

"The lady who brings Maia every morning."

"Oh, that's her mother."

"Well, then who's the man—the one who takes her home?" continued Johnny uncertainly, with confusion in his voice.

"That's her father," the teacher replied automatically.

"But they aren't the same . . . ."

"That's true," said the teacher, suddenly realizing Johnny's confusion and trying to quickly come up with an answer that would make sense.

Before she could respond, Johnny interjected, "But Maia's not Black like her mother. Is she Black; or is she White, like her daddy?"

Children of mixed racial and ethnic backgrounds are an ever-increasing phenomenon in early childhood programs. These children are products of parents who have gone outside conventional identity groups to marry. Because of more interaction between different people in social, work, and school settings, more and more marriages occur outside conventionally held options. Blacks marry Whites; Hispanics, Whites; Asians, Blacks; and so on. Children from these unions have unique problems that must be addressed by early childhood programs.

These children add to the richness of the early childhood experience for all of the children in the child care setting, but teachers and administrators are often as confused as Johnny. Are these children Black, or are they White? Are they Hispanic? Are they Asian, or are they just American? Or, as Maia—a pretty, vivacious four-year-old with two little braids, an upturned nose, and sparkling eyes set in a round face—would have answered: "Mummy's Black, daddy's White, and I'm Brown."

I am Maia's father, an Englishman with black curly hair, brown eyes, and a proclivity for athletics and dance. Whenever people attribute Maia's hair, dark eyes, and balletic gymnastic skill to her Black mother, I get incensed. My four children have the strength of both cultures, and not necessarily according to stereotypical standards. Conventional thinking labeled any person with any Black heritage as being Black, any child of a White parent and one non-Black parent as also being Black. While much of society still holds to these categories, and some parents of interracial children do, many parents of children of combined heritage subscribe to the idea that their children are products of both parents' heritages, and their identity should reflect this clear heritage.

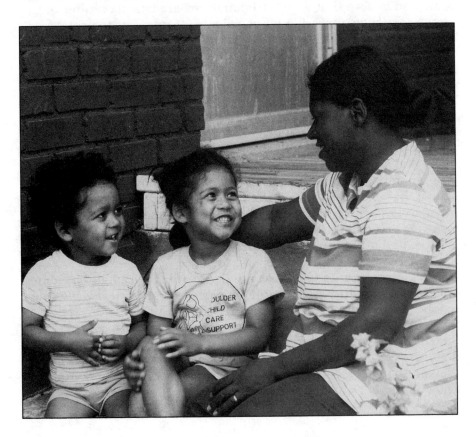

Terminology

There are various viewpoints about the terminology to be used to describe children of interracial families: interracial, biracial, mixed, brown, and rainbow have all been suggested. The term *interracial* is used because it is inclusive of families with a variety of heritages: African, European, Asian, Native American, Hispanic, etc. (Shackford, 1984)

Support the identity of interracial children

Professionals working with young interracial children must consider three general directions in working with these children.

Their own deep-seated beliefs about this issue

Interracial relationships are contaminated by a history of racism and an overanalysis of the evils involved. Unfortunately some professionals working with young children are uneasy with this issue and believe that all mixed marriages are based on ulterior motives, such as marrying for social advancement or to protest society's racial prejudices. Staff should openly explore this issue, maybe with a professional leader who can sort out the feelings, attitudes, and prejudices.

The views of the child's parents

Parents of interracial children set the tone for that child's identity. Many of these parents will be struggling with the question at home and with their relatives and friends. Ultimately, though, the program must support the parents' views. A conference before school that explores the issue of the child's identity is, therefore, a must. Talk to the parents openly and nonjudgmentally about the issue of their child's identity. Suggest reading materials, support groups, and other interracial parents in the program who might help the parents sort out their own feelings.

Don't force parents to choose an identity for their child based on one parent's identity or conventional societal categories. While the teacher must support the parents' wishes on this issue, the teacher should also assist the parents in exploring the entire question of identity. Many interracial parents have not come to a definitive feeling on this issue. They often feel isolated and believe they must use the conventional identity categories. Let parents know that other choices are available.

The importance of a child's sense of identity to the child's overall development

How parents and teachers respond when children come to them with questions is of great importance in shaping that child's self-image. "My friend Mike is Black, Gene is White. What am I?" "Jimmy (who is Hispanic) says I'm Black, and he isn't. But he's darker than me. Why?" These questions were asked by Maia when she was four years old. We know that young children are very interested about themselves—their name, parents, hair, size, age—and how they fit in with other children. Teachers must be ever aware and sensitive to each child's need to feel good about his physical appearance, physical and intellectual abilities, and family heritage.

But don't stereotype! "You're a good dancer like your mother (because she's Black)." "You have curly hair like your daddy (because he's Black)." "Your blue eyes are like your mummy (who is White)." Children want to know they are like their father and mother because their father and mother are their parents, not because all Blacks have curly hair, all Whites have blue eyes, or all Asians are good at math!

Early childhood programs must support interracial families

All families of young children today are under extreme pressure: ever-increasing cost of raising children; need for both parents to work; selecting and monitoring of child care; antichild mood in the country today; negative influence of television; prevalence of one-parent homes; fear of kidnapping and strangers; and loss of antipoverty programs. Interracial families have a particular kind of stress: new interracial families must struggle with the nation's rejection of the concepts and ideas that brought the family together.

In their daily lives parents of interracial children must face racism constantly; many have also lost the financial and practical support of parents and grandparents on both sides of the family. They often feel that they are fighting a long battle against relatives who don't want them and a country that has gone back on its commitment to equality for all people.

The early childhood program can become a setting where much of this stress is alleviated, where interracial families can find new friends and helpers who will support them in their struggle and who can tap into systems to fill the gap left by estranged relatives. Interracial couples are as serious as any other couple about raising healthy, well-developed children; they should be helped and supported by the school in this effort. Parents of interracial children should feel that the school is an active advocate and supporter of their desire to provide a good home and a good education for their children.

The early childhood program is one of the first settings where children must survive being different and come to grips with the often cruel world. Interracial children are, physically, so obviously different. This means that the adult who is racially biased will pick on these children, and other children who are unusually curious about physical differences will pick on them. When a child is in an argument, he will find the first thing he can to make the other child seem inferior. If the other child is obviously interracial, that's what will be used. Other differences between children are less physically apparent and therefore are less likely to be used.

Early childhood programs should take advantage of the richness of interracial children

Children of interracial heritage add a great deal to the richness and quality of the school setting. They bring at least two distinctive cultures; they have experience of dance, art, language, and culture richer than most children; and they have a broad base of knowledge. They play easily with children in the program from diverse backgrounds, and they bring an openness to the setting. Obviously, this richness and diversity will be evident and will be an attribute to the program only if it is recognized, encouraged, and supported.

Eirlys, my six-year-old, knows that her heritage includes Black, English, Native American, and Oriental. Thus, when her class studies the food, culture, dress, or geography of those peoples, Erica has a personal interest and enthusiasm. She talks to her class about her English grandfather; her Black grandfather, who still lives in Kansas City; and her Indian heritage. She is also enthusiastic about any different background and heritage. This openness to a cosmopolitan approach can be effectively used by teachers and picked up by other children. Most interracial children have a doubly rich heritage and life experience that can be an asset to the classroom. Other children will learn an enjoyment of people who look different and who have a different heritage.

Interracial children also challenge the temptation for teachers and children to divide the child care experience into Black and White: Black and White dolls; Black and White pictures; Black and White fairy tales, histories, and festivals. They force the program to address the richness of all cultures that color the human existence; they encourage other children to realize that they cannot place all people into one of two either/or categories: Black or White, rich or poor, friend or enemy.

"Well, what are you anyway, Black or White?" asked the six-year-old of her schoolmate Maia.

"Actually, my daddy's English and my mummy's part Black and part Indian, and there's some Japanese in me somewhere . . . ."

"Oh, that's okay," interrupted the curious girl, "I'm sorry I asked."

This kind of interaction forces a child to think about racial categories, about placing other children into neat little boxes. When Eirlys did a picture of her family, she cut and pasted a Black

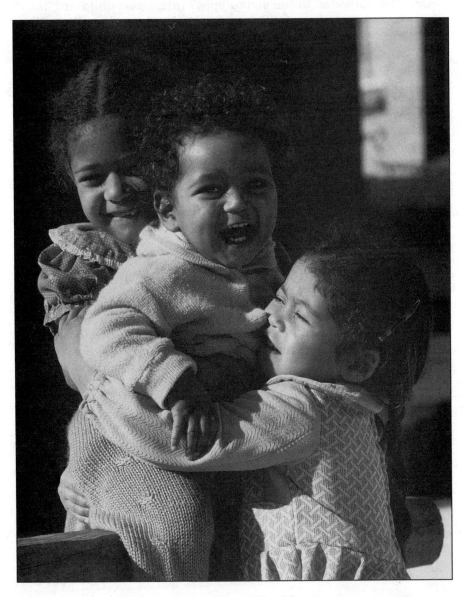

woman for her mother, a White man for her father, two light-skinned Blacks for her sister and brother (there are very few biracial models), then used a brown crayon to draw a baby because she could find no photos of babies with a skin color like her own. In a program that understands and appreciates the richness of people's heritages and the dangers of placing people into cultural and racial stereotypical categories, efforts like this by interracial children add tremendously to the richness and cosmopolitan approach of the curriculum.

And what happens to the stereotypes? Interracial children, like other children, can be intelligent, beautiful, athletic, or gifted; they can enjoy music and dance. (Mine are all of the above!)

From my experience knowing many interracial families, many of these parents are very concerned about their children's upbringing. They know that they have challenged conventional attitudes, and they want to make sure that their children will not suffer. They have thought a great deal about how they want to raise their children, so they often become actively involved in their children's education and child care programs. Parents will work to keep a program sensitive to their needs and to their children's needs and demand that teachers reflect their feelings and attitudes toward their interracial children. A strong program that supports children and families of mixed racial and ethnic backgrounds will send a clear message to prospective parents about the program's policies.

Specific ideas for teachers

In working with these families, teachers and administrators must understand that interracial families are as different from each other as are any other families. They cover the whole range of economic, religious, educational, and value differences. Their children are as different as any other children from different homes. They cannot be stereotyped.

Teachers must be sensitive to children as individual personalities made up of varied and rich backgrounds. But even as they are aware of the multiheritage of a child's background, they must be watchful of the traps.

Recently my three-year-old, Kealan, and I were watching the World Cup soccer games. Kealan kept asking, "Who's the black man?" I noticed one of the teams was from Morocco, so I said, "The Black men play for an African team. Some people from Africa are Black." He was not satisfied and kept asking. Finally he pointed to the television, asking, "That black man?" He was pointing to the referee, who was dressed in black!

While it's critical to understand the child's interracial heritage and to be sensitive to his use of it in daily activities within the classroom, remember that the majority of his experiences will be like those of any other child—with little apparent reference to his interracial heritage.

• Meet with the parent(s) before each school year and regularly during the year. During these meetings discuss, along with issues that affect all parents and children, how the parents deal with their children's heritage and how they want the school to support it. How do they respond to racist remarks to their children? What do they say to their children?

• Include curriculum materials showing people of mixed racial and ethnic backgrounds. This should include children's books (see "Reflecting Diversity—Books to Read with Young Children" on p. 163) and pictures of biracial children and interracial couples, historical people of mixed racial and ethnic backgrounds, and current interracial heroes.

• While studying people, cultures, art, and dance, avoid breaking the world into racial groupings. Stress individuals; focus on how art, music, and dance transcend national, geographic, and racial boundaries.

• Allow for open and supportive questions about race, color, hair texture, heritage, and identity. Just as a four-year-old will ask, "Am I older than you?" and "Who's biggest?," they will ask, "Are you Black?" "Is your mother Mexican?" and "Am I darker than you?" When these questions come up, remember what the child's parent has said about the child's identity, and respond in terms of everyone having a rich heritage (Italian, German, Native American, Chinese, African, and so forth). Remember that children are naturally very curious and don't want a deep explanation for what they see as simple physical characteristics. Obviously, the teacher must be comfortable with these discussions.

• Allow children of different racial and ethnic backgrounds to play in the housekeeping corner as married couples. If other children comment, use this as an opportunity to talk about the naturalness of different people—national, religious, and racial—marrying. Be positive.

• Help biracial and multiethnic children to feel proud of their heritage. Help them to identify other biracial and multiethnic children in the program, or a biracial staff person, or biracial people in pictures or materials in the classroom. Help them draw people like themselves, provide dolls that are like them, and encourage them to impose their physical features into pretend play and art activities. Don't try to avoid the issue.

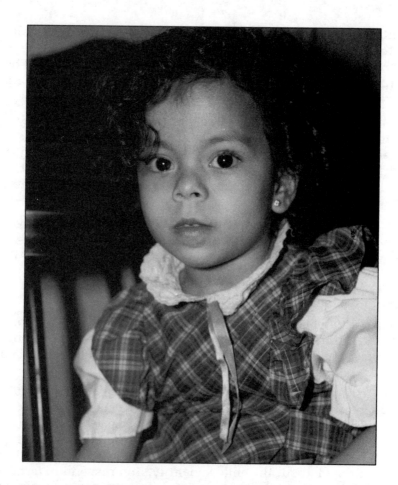

• Use interracial children's experiences and heritage to expand activities for all of the children. Discussion on interracial heritage can include national heritage of all children, religious combinations, and interesting physical attributes: "Where did you get your green eyes and red hair?" "Was your grandfather so tall?"

Have children bring in pictures of their relatives. Discuss the countries children came from, the languages, and the customs. Have parents and grandparents visit the program and talk about their lives. Use children whose parents are different to discuss differences, how all children respond to them, how differences should not be feared, and how learning about differences can be fun.

• Help these children stand up to children and adults who attack their identity. Help them protect themselves and retain their pride.

• Help these children to understand that some people see them as different, that it's okay to be different, and that many of the great people of the world are proud to be different.

• Try to expose these children to role models. Invite interracial couples to your program; encourage a variety of teachers and volunteers; mix older multiracial and multiethnic children with younger children.

• Understand that most of these children's problems and their parents' problems have nothing to do with their mixed heritage. It is too simple to ascribe problems to their unique heritage, and doing so will encourage these children to use their background as an excuse.

• A child's positive identity at this age is directly tied to how he feels about his physical characteristics, how he feels about his family and his friends, and what he can do (art, music, reading, climbing, and so forth). So the most important thing that the program and its staff can do is to make the interracial child and his family totally accepted in the program. The child must feel positive about his physical features; the parent(s) must feel accepted and supported when they visit; the child must feel good about a particular accomplishment because *he* did it.

Interracial children and their families provide a rich contribution to early childhood programs. They bring a multiplicity of experiences, knowledge, and exposure to the program. These additions should be effectively used by program staff to enhance learning for other children, to support the richness of diversity and difference, and to enrich the entire curriculum. The program should also take advantage of interracial parents' efforts and interest in their children's development to strengthen the program.

For further reading

Aldridge, D. (1978). Interracial marriage: Empirical and theoretical consequences. *Journal of Black Studies, 8* (3), 355–368.

Baptiste, P. (1983, December). Rearing the interracial child. *Communique,* 4–5.

Baptiste, P. (1985, April). The contemporary interracial child. *Communique,* 1–7.

Children of Interracial Families. (1984). *Interracial Books for Children Bulletin,* 15(6).

Wardle, F. (1987). Are you sensitive to interracial children's special identity needs? *Young Children, 42*(2), 53–59.

Wardle, F. (1985, Fall). Mummy's black, Daddy's white, and I'm brown. *Communique,* 4–7.

Wardle, F. (1984, September). Please check one—White, black, other, mixed. *Communique,* 2–3.

Reference

Shackford, K. (1984). Interracial children: Growing up healthy in an unhealthy society. *Interracial Books for Children Bulletin,* 15(6), 4–6.

FRANCIS WARDLE is director of the Adams County, Colorado, Head Start and Day Care, the father of four biracial children, and director of the Study of Biracial Children.

Parenting a Child With Special Needs

An interview with Meg Robinson

What is it like for parents when their child has a disability?

When you have a child who has a disability, there's a lot that goes on. You go through the same stages you go through in any kind of difficult situation. First you have denial of the problem; every parent has denial in varying degrees. Then you want to hide it, make it a secret. No one should know that my child has a disability, that my child is going to be labeled. Then you have to try to deal with what the implications of the disability are for the child, for you as the parent of the child, for the school, and so on. And it's not as if you go through all of those adjustments and then wrap it up and put it on a shelf. The adjustment is ongoing—there are peaks and plateaus; you gradually reach some hurdles and you get over them.

I sound very negative; I'm actually very positive. You gain a lot, too. Raising a child with disabilities helps you become a more sensitive person, more aware of other people. I'm certainly more sensitive to anyone who has a disability as a result of having a child with that sort of problem. And the child subtly develops other strengths as a means of compensating for having the disability— and those strengths can be very rewarding.

How can early childhood teachers help parents as they go through these adjustments?

Here is the issue for educators. A lot of times, up until the child is two or three years of age, the parents may not know that there is a defined disability (sometimes parents may not know until the child is in kindergarten or even older). The whole process of diagnosing what problems may be there is a long, frustrating, and sometimes threatening process to go through. Often the teacher, particularly in the early years, figures out what the strengths of the child are, what the weaknesses are, and if there are defined areas where the child needs help.

Part of the problem is diagnostic. A teacher is not a physician, and you don't want the teacher to be placed in the position of feeling that she's responsible for diagnosing potential problems, whatever they may be. You don't want a teacher to look at every child as a diagnostic puzzle. In preschool a lot of things can emerge, and the earlier they are diagnosed, the better. It's easier to face that challenge when the child is five years old than when he is seven or eight.

The whole diagnostic process, then, is one that needs to be a team effort. It should start, certainly, with the parents; however, if there is a strong element of denial, the teacher can play an important role in persuading the parents (if there is a problem) that the child needs to be tested, receive physical therapy, or whatever.

How can teachers most effectively communicate this kind of information?

It's really tough. It's always hard when you're a parent to listen to any problem connected with your child. The teacher is an authority figure for a parent, and what she says carries a lot of weight. In listening to a teacher talk about a child, it's helpful to parents if the following is taken into consideration:

• It's done on a one-to-one, sit-down level in a nonthreatening way.

• It takes place in person.

• The child is first discussed as an individual with many strengths. It's good for the parent to know what the teacher likes about the child. Things should be discussed in a constructive way.

• Words that would be potentially threatening should be avoided.

• Diplomacy is important. The teacher can suggest without coming down hard, without saying that such and such is a problem. For example, teachers could say things like, "We see your child in just one of the many environments that he's in. These are just our observations. You, the parents, know him better than we do; we're just giving you some input. We do have the advantage of seeing 20 children his age and stage every year, and you only have the opportunity of knowing him and a few other children his age. So we have that vantage point from which to share information with you." If the teacher approaches the subject from that standpoint, it's less threatening to the parent.

The other side of it is that the teacher has to level with the parent. If there is a problem, the parents need to know about it and do something to resolve it.

My child, David, has mild cerebral palsy. He wasn't walking at 18 or 19 months—but I was a late walker, so we didn't think one way or the other about it. I had a friend who said, "Look, David really should be checked out. He really looks like he might have a problem. Call . . . ." But there was a lot of denial there.

We took him to many doctors to figure out what the problem was. I had a terrible experience when I was sent to see an orthopedist who said to a resident, "Oh, this child obviously has mild cerebral palsy." I'd never heard the words cerebral palsy applied to my child! It was very difficult.

Then we thought, "We're not going to tell anybody because it will be a problem." But *we* were the ones who had the problem. We were the ones who were threatened, and it was that, more than the fact that we were trying to protect David, that made us want to keep the problem quiet.

After David was diagnosed, a neighbor who was a priest suggested that we call St. Columba's because they have such a wonderful program that includes children with special needs.

How can teachers work with parents to provide the best experiences for children?

After the diagnosis, you get to the point of using an integrative approach. There are a lot of people who know the child in many different ways—teachers, parents, doctors, and therapists. One of the tricks is to act as a catalyst to bring all of these people together and to be the conduit of information that flows back and forth. All of these people have something to contribute and something to gain from listening to the others.

Even though St. Columba's has scheduled sessions with parents and teachers, I bring in the therapists, who talk about how David is doing and give each other suggestions: "Here's where David needs to be challenged" or "Don't push him in this area." And I send the doctor's reports to the school so that the teachers are filled in and understand everything that's happening.

It's the parents' role to be the catalyst because parents are the only ones who know all of the players, but if the parents don't pick up on this responsibility, the teacher may try to play that role. The one big barrier the teacher has is if the parents are unwilling for whatever reason—they feel threatened, or they don't want to spend the time, or whatever—to pull all this information together. It's very difficult for teachers to go beyond a certain point, but they can encourage it to happen: "We know that David is getting therapy. Could you send me any reports that the therapist has done, like some progress reports on how he's doing?"

The other approach teachers can take is to have parents get together and share some of these things. Maybe it's less threatening in a group than it is one-to-one. With any kind of problem, it's helpful to know that someone else has the same problem and to try to develop strategies together and learn from each other.

Last year, my husband, Jody, and I started a parenting group with parents from St. Columba's who have children with identified special needs. We met once a month for six or seven sessions and covered a multitude of issues. Even though it was very beneficial for Jody and me and it worked out pretty well, we are not doing it this year. Once we went beyond a certain point, the issues became fragmented. The nature of the disability, the severity of the disability, how the child coped, how the parents coped—all made the needs so diverse that we decided to take a different approach this year. This year there is a parenting group covering broader issues,

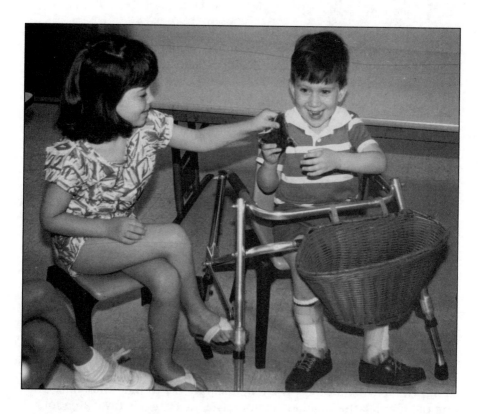

and within that context there may be a session that deals with parenting children with disabilities.

What things can an early childhood program do to bolster you as a parent?

At St. Columba's they have on their staff, as consultants, special education people who come in periodically to observe and to give feedback to the teachers. So there are other professionals that teachers can turn to and people that teachers can draw into talking with parents. They're also available for parents. I found the professionals to be very helpful, both from a technical standpoint and for psychological support.

St. Columba's looks at the child in a holistic way. They really home in on the child's strengths, capabilities, and potential. The child is encouraged to pursue avenues that will strengthen her as a person and allow her to grow. The teachers transmit their discoveries to parents, and parents come away looking at their child a little bit differently.

We've grown a lot during the three years David has been at St. Columba's Nursery School. When he started the program, I think we pampered him. I worked full time and we had a person full time taking care of him. She was wonderful and loving and, because of her great affection for David, she didn't push him quite as much as she could have. When we started St. Columba's, it was like night and day. They expected him to get his coat on, to take his coat off, to unsnap his pants when he went to the bathroom, and that sort of thing. And they said to us, very gently but very clearly, "Look, David can be doing more things than he's doing. He can put his coat on and take it off. We'll show you the way." They insisted on our challenging him more; and they did it by saying, "We know that David can do such and such, and you should begin to insist that he do some of these things at home." That was very helpful.

When David was there the first year, I didn't really have the time to get very involved with things that were going on at the school. The staff never put pressure on me to get involved. Now I am thinking that maybe they should have encouraged me to spend more time in the school, but that's really not their role. I was being a good mother. The program has to accept the realities within each family. One mother may have more time to spend with her child than another has. It's important for parents to know that teachers are not standing in judgment of them.

What do you think the program is like for your son?

There are 2 children with special needs in each class of 18 children. The structure is multifaceted—they don't stress just academics, just motor skills, or just psychological development. The main objective is to make the children feel good about themselves and to bolster confidence and a sense of curiosity about themselves, other people, and their environment. The teachers do it by being positive, by having an enthusiastic outlook. It's very contagious.

David, during the first year, was very shy. He wasn't sure of himself. Motorwise, he was very limited in what he would try to do. Over the three years, he's become much more outgoing, much more confident. He tries to do a lot more things, and the teachers have encouraged him to try and not to worry if he fails. The trick is to try and if you fail, that's okay—you just get up and keep going. I think they've made him much more resilient in a lot of ways—personally, with others, motorwise; he's motivated to experiment.

They're very loving. It's one thing to challenge a child and try to encourage a child to try different things, but then you need to be there to have that net of support if the child needs to fall back or needs that reassurance. So you need to both challenge and support. If you do only one or the other, it's not good. You need a balance.

The challenge for the teacher is to treat each child as an individual, to seek differences, and to be equitable. If you treat everyone the same, you are not making use of each child's uniqueness. So you need to seek and recognize the differences and to help the child feel comfortable with her own differences. The goal is to develop an appreciation for each child as an individual and then to help parents value their child as an individual.

Having a disabled child presents a lot of challenges. It really tests the strengths of the parents and the child, and forces all who are involved to come to terms with being different and what that really means. The disability that at first seems so significant, somewhat embarrassing, and difficult to acknowledge slowly diminishes in importance as the individuality of the child emerges. David is witty, loving, bright, autonomous, and headstrong. I don't know to what extent his cerebral palsy has influenced his personality, but it is one of many facets of his life.

The disability will always be there. He once asked if he will always have cerebral palsy. I told him, "Yes, but it will improve through therapy and your own ability to deal with it." He cried about it, and I cried with him because it was a sad reality for us both. This was a year ago, and I think that moment was a turning point. Openly acknowledging the disability has been helpful for all of us, and it must remain an open subject. However, everyone in the family feels that the disability is not the main focus or characteristic that defines David or that defines our role as his parents.

The issue of David's disability cannot be resolved at any one stage because at each phase of development implications of the cerebral palsy will present themselves in different forms. However, my husband and I believe that our job is to make David feel good about himself, to make him feel that he can accomplish almost anything he sets his mind to, and to assure him that we will be there if he needs us.

At the time of this book's original publication, MEG ROBINSON was a free-lance consultant specializing in marketing, strategic planning, and microcomputers. Meg is a mother of four boys. Her son David, who has mild cerebral palsy, is now 11 years old, Joshua is 7, Micah is 5, and Noah is 1. Meg, a singer/songwriter performing under the name Potomac Red, is releasing a new recording for children 6 to 12 years of age.

Chapter 5
LIVING IN A CHANGING WORLD

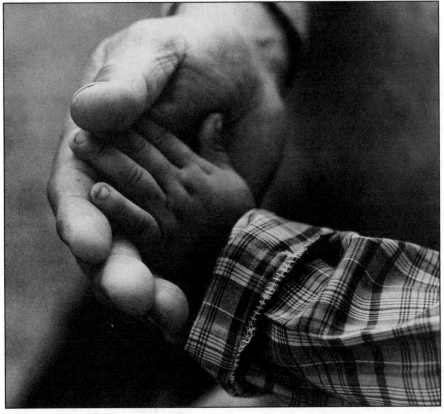

"I don't think I'm different."

—*Richard Koen*
in *The Wall Street Journal*
January 16, 1987

The Impact of Current Changes in Social Structure on Early Childhood Education Programs

Gail Raymond and Dean K. McIntosh

Mrs. Williams has decided to return to preschool teaching after a 15-year absence. On her first day in the classroom, she arrives at 6:45 because she is anxious to be the first one there. Her initial shock is to find two three-year-olds sitting patiently on the front step of the school. Their parents, both working mothers, left the children there at 6:30 so they could be to work on time.

Recovering from this shock (this never would have happened 15 years ago), she goes inside with the arriving staff. Much to her surprise, the next three children to arrive are all immigrant and refugee children who speak no English, nor do their parents. Another child is brought in by an elderly grandparent who has sole responsibility for the child during the day, as he is retired and the mother has moved home after a recent divorce.

Finally, things feel normal again, as several middle-class children arrive who are more like the children she remembers. However, the next child to arrive is not dressed properly, smells bad, and has a cold. Mrs. Williams looks for the mother, but learns that the child has been transported and left at the doorstep by a social service agency.

As the morning progresses, Mrs. Williams discovers that the children come from a mixture of low-, middle-, and upper-middle-income families. They are of various ethnic backgrounds, some speak no English, some have mothers who are in their teens, and many come from single-parent homes. She feels as if she is in a time warp; but, no, she has entered the present day and real world of early childhood education.

During recent years this country has experienced dramatic modifications in social structure. The size and composition of socioeconomic classes have changed markedly, with concomitant changes in family structure. Whereas early childhood programs traditionally have been developed on the basis of a stereotyped middle-class perspective on society and the family, this approach must now be reexamined in light of contemporary social changes.

Current changes in social structure

Many educators continue to view children in terms of traditionally assumed socioeconomic groupings. Even as late as the mid-1960s, there were three well-defined levels reported in the literature and used by most economists and sociologists—lower, middle, and upper classes, with differentiation usually based upon combinations of factors such as personal income, place of residence, profession, and educational background. During recent years, however, these classes have changed dramatically in size and structure due to rapid technological changes, civil rights and feminist movements, population shifts, expansion of mass communications, and job relocation, to name just a few of the causative factors. These changes have resulted in a shrinking of the middle class and an expansion of the lower class, with the poor becoming even poorer.

Even though these changes in social class structure have occurred, schools in general have failed to respond to these shifts

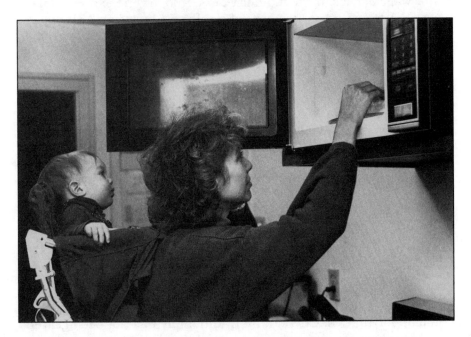

and continue to function under the "middle-class syndrome"—for the most part, teachers, the curriculum in the schools, and even the schools' philosophy reflect the emphasis found in the traditional middle class of the 1960s. Middle class has served as a hallmark and standard for the rest of society almost from the beginning of these United States.

To this day educators have long-standing preconceived ideas regarding the make-up of each of these three economic levels; these beliefs, in turn, have influenced the overall approach used in providing education to all children. The **low-income** family is stereotypically viewed as one in which poverty is evident; there is often an unmarried mother, and a stable male model is usually absent. There are many children at home whose age range may be quite large. The house is usually substandard and most often is rented from an absentee landlord who cares little about keeping up the structure. Medical care and overall health of the children tend to be much below that of children in other socioeconomic groups because the parents must depend upon *free* medical care, which involves numerous confusing forms to fill out and long waiting lines. There is little or no hope for the future as the poverty tends to be self-perpetuating. Low-income individuals are seen as lacking skills and educational opportunities that lead to economic opportunity. Their fight to survive on a day-to-day basis consumes all available energy.

The stereotype of the **middle class** is primarily of the two-parent family, with both parents living at home and the father being the major wage earner. If the mother works, it is for one express purpose—to help with the expenses of a college education. Although there are several income levels within the middle class, all of the parents share the same dream of a better life for their children. Economic opportunity, for this group, is unalterably linked to a college education. It is presumed that a better life with more money is the goal of most middle-class parents.

The **upper-class** stereotype is the fortunate few who are free from economic worry. The lives of both of the parents are filled with many civic and philanthropic activities, all of which take both time and money. Upper-class children are believed to be raised by full-time housekeepers or regularly employed babysitters. They attend elite public or private schools and are expected to carry on the family name and tradition.

Since the beginning of free public education in the United States, teachers have held these concepts of social structure and have geared education primarily to the middle class. Educators have considered the middle class to be the primary supporter of schools, both emotionally and through taxes, and the middle class has been seen as the main beneficiary of public-provided educational opportunities. Curriculum traditionally has not been geared

Income Statistics

Rose (S. J. Rose, *The American Profile Poster*, New York: Pantheon Books, 1986) has demonstrated that the middle class has diminished markedly between 1978 and 1986, with 2.8% of that group entering the *high-budget* group and 5.2% moving into the *low-budget* and *poverty* groups. Families with children have constituted the bulk of those Americans moving into the poorer socioeconomic class.

Rose also pointed out that there has been a sharp income redistribution from poor to rich among families with children between 1968 and 1983, with the lowest fifth of families with children receiving 7.4% of cash family incomes in 1968 and 4.8% in 1983, and the highest fifth receiving 33.8% in 1968 and 38.1% in 1983.

The number of low-income children jumped 30% between 1979 and 1984, while their participation in two key federal programs dropped sharply during the same period. The rate of participation in Head Start and Aid to Families with Dependent Children (AFDC) fell more than 20% during this five-year period, and the number of low-income children jumped from 9.9 million to 12.9 million ("Study Says Young Poor Count Up," *The State*, October 1986, p. 14.). Stated differently, 22% of all children now reside in households with an income below the poverty line, whereas during the 1970s the poverty rate for children remained between 14 and 16%.

the needs of the lower class, as the idea has been to educate this group to move into the middle class of society. The upper class was not considered to need the attention of the public schools, as many of the children attended private schools. Those upper-class children who attended public schools were in the *better* schools in the district, in which the curriculum and extracurricular experiences were rich and varied. In addition, their economic status was guaranteed, and they would benefit little from a formal education unlike the middle- and lower-class students.

These preconceived ideas of social class composition and class-related educational needs are not consistent with the realities of the mid-1980s. The boundaries between these groups have begun to change as the middle class has shrunk, the lower class has expanded, and the poor have become even more destitute. As rapid social mobility has occurred, the composition of each class has changed, and traditional stereotypes of classes do not fit.

Changes in socioeconomic status can occur rapidly (see box above). The following case examples demonstrate the rapidity of social mobility—potentially in either direction, although more often downward.

A middle-income steel worker in a middle-class community has worked for a local textile/steel mill since he graduated from high school. He is 35 years of age with four children, the youngest 2 years old and the oldest 16. One Friday he receives notification that his job will be abolished the following Friday. Overnight the family moves from middle income to lower income, and they may soon appear on the welfare rolls for an extended period of time, as they have little in savings. This man has only specialized skills learned in the mill over the last 17 years, and he lacks the fundamental educational skills needed to participate successfully in a retraining program.

A different example is the 37-year-old wife of a professional man. She and her husband live in an upper-income golf club community. She is told by her husband that he is filing for divorce. They have three children, ages 6 months to 10 years. She holds a master's degree in English literature, received 13 years ago. She has never been employed outside the home. The family, although in the upper-income level, has limited savings and few investments other than the home, which has little equity in it. She is forced to move the children into a two-bedroom apartment while she seeks employment. She quickly realizes that her degree earned many years ago is useless in today's business world. The child support provided by the father barely meets the essentials for the daily living standard acquired over the past 13 years. She has found herself, probably permanently, in the lower-middle-income group. The type of employment immediately available to her will be close to minimum wage in a position that will allow little, if any, upward economic and social mobility in the near future.

A third example is the career-oriented couple. The father is a business executive and the mother an account executive with a local advertising firm. The jobs of both demand extremely long hours of work each day. In addition, extended periods of business travel, entertaining of clients, and being visible at civic functions are all part of the job responsibilities. Their child attends an expensive child care program and spends many evenings and weekends with babysitters. Both parents are well aware of the need to be *good parents* and they try, whenever possible, to spend time with their child. Both are big believers in *quality time*, in which what limited time is available is well organized and intensive. Unfortunately, they fail to realize that *quantity time* is also important. This upwardly mobile, and rapidly growing, segment of today's society of career-oriented parents too often lacks both the time and the energy to be interested in anything more than the child's overall academic development.

Such changes in socioeconomic status, for better or worse, often take place abruptly and dramatically, allowing the family little time to make any preparations for the changes. For a vast majority, any change of economic level is going to be negative and often irreversible, or at least long-term in nature. While the move up the economic ladder is often slow, the move down can be rapid and catastrophic in its impact upon the family structure.

The data and realities refute traditionally held assumptions about society that have influenced early childhood education programs today. It is inappropriate for a preschool teacher to subscribe to the traditional *middle-class orientation* and to structure her teaching of all children around this focus. There are several problems with this traditional approach. First, it was *never* valid to stereotype children from certain classes and assume that they had certain strengths or weaknesses based on their background and environment. While lower-income children may lack opportunities that are available to other children, each child must be seen as an autonomous person, and his or her abilities must be individually assessed. Second, with the shrinking of the middle

---

Changes in U.S. Households

By the year 2000, one-third of all people in the United States will be non-White (C.G. Williams, "Population Trends Affect Education," *South Carolina School Board's Association Journal*, 1986, pp. 20–21).

Currently 20% of all children live in female-headed households (U.S. Bureau of the Census, *Marital Status and Living Arrangements—Current Population Report* [Series p. 20, No. 52], Washington, DC: Author, March 1981). Three-fifths (60%) of all children born in 1986 will spend at least part of their lives in a single-parent family, with 90% of these being headed by females ("Deceptive Picture: Despite Signs to the Contrary, A Comeback by the Old Style Family Isn't Likely," *The Wall Street Journal*, September 1986, p. 22).

One-fifth (21.5%) of all children born in 1985 were born to unmarried mothers, compared to 7.7% in 1965. The rate is rapidly increasing, especially with teenage pregnancies ("Deceptive Picture," 1986).

By the year 1990, the traditional family—consisting of a working father, a full-time housewife mother, and two or more children—will constitute only 6% of families [L.G. Baruth and M.Z. Burggraf, "The Counselor and Single Parent Families," *Elementary School Guidance and Counseling*, 19 (1), 1984, pp. 30–37].

Poverty has rapidly become feminized, with 57% of Americans officially in poverty being female. There are now 3.6 million low-income families with a female head of household, up 82% from 1960 (Rose, 1986).

class, more and more children are entering the lower socioeconomic group; it would be irrelevant to teach all children using an approach geared to a fictional middle-class group of children. With busing across neighborhoods and with the quick shifting of entire groups of children into lower income groups, few teachers have a purely middle-class group of students. Third, with the fluid nature of today's society, even if a teacher has a group of predominantly middle-class children at the beginning of the year, this ratio could change by the end of the year. For example, an industry's closing could send entire school districts into poverty.

In addition to these social class shifts that have occurred in recent years, there are other contemporary trends in family structure that have implications for preschool teachers. These changes also repudiate the use of a middle-class perspective in developing early childhood programs. The structure of the American family is changing, and it is not appropriate for teachers to view children in terms of traditional stereotypical ideas of the family. While some of these changes in family structure may be in opposition to the presently held values of educators, the educators should be aware of these developments and take them into consideration when planning curricula. Many of these trends have been known for the past 10 years, yet educators have done little to address the impact of these trends when planning early childhood programs.

These changes in social class structure and the current trends in family composition suggest that preschool teachers may need to modify some of their theoretical perspectives and, consequently, change some of their approaches to teaching. The use of a middle-class perspective in designing and implementing preschool programs is not valid, and teachers must develop their programs in light of current changes in social class and family structure.

Implications for early childhood programs

The changes in social class and family composition described above should influence the design of curriculum for early childhood programs as well as the approaches used in assessing the strengths, weaknesses, and needs of each individual child.

Curriculum design. If, by the year 2000, one-third of all United States residents will be non-White, it is very important for early childhood programs to expose children to various ethnic groups through real-life experiences and program content and materials. In California, for example, all children need great amounts of exposure to Latinos and their way of life. Early and positive exposure to many ethnic groups is essential to help children become

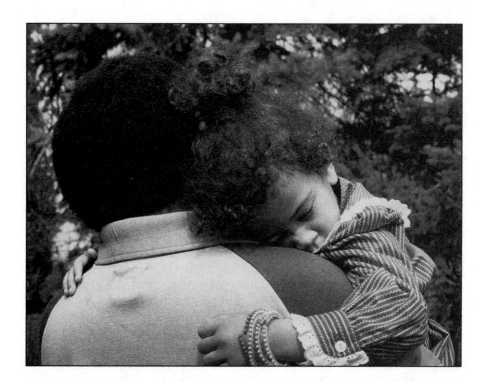

aware of the ethnic groups around them and their relationship to other ethnic groups.

In addition to the increase of non-White citizens, there continues to be an influx of immigrant and refugee children from all parts of the world, especially Southeast Asia and South and Central America. The parents know the importance of education and of becoming a part of the system, so they quickly place their children in available preschool programs. Many of these children speak no English when they enter a program, and their parents speak little more than rudimentary English. Teachers face the necessity of gaining skills in teaching English to non-English-speaking children. They must also work with these parents regarding the type of education offered to young children, for it may be very different from the expectations they had for their children in their native countries.

The teacher can seek experts within the community who have in-depth knowledge about the various cultures and ethnic groups that are represented within the classroom—for example, church members who are involved in sponsoring refugees from Southeast Asia. Experts within social service agencies or local colleges and universities, and the parents themselves, are also resources.

With approximately 60% of all children facing the prospect of living in single-parent homes—most often with their mothers—the curriculum should be designed to assist these children in validating their family situation. Far too often young children only hear about and see representations of the traditional family situation, which makes it extremely difficult for them to understand how their own family situation correlates with what they are hearing and seeing.

By the same token, if males are becoming less present and involved within certain family structures, it is important that children of both sexes be provided with positive male images and role models at this early age. Male guests and helpers and the presence of men as teachers in child care programs are all needed. There is also the need to select materials that reinforce images of men, as well as women, in a broad spectrum of roles.

Stepparents and grandparents are playing increasingly significant caretaking roles in the lives of many young children. It may be that the only feasible economic solution for a separated and/or divorced parent is to return home to parents. Grandparents may have to assume the major responsibility for raising the grandchildren while the parent works. Regardless of the situation, positive images of stepparents and grandparents should be present in materials and curriculum.

Increasing numbers of children of teenage mothers will be present in preschool programs, and it becomes necessary to involve the teenage mothers in the educational process in a different way. Many of these mothers will reside in homes in which there are no adult males and in which the mother of the teenager may also have very young children. It may well be that neither of the two ever gained the skills of motherhood, thus there is no passing down of these skills. The preschool teacher can assume a significant role in assisting these young mothers in developing good parenting skills.

Informal assessment. Socioeconomic factors have an impact on all children even before they come to school; however, most children still arrive ready and excited to learn. They bring their own experiences from the home and community, which may be rich and varied or extremely limited. Nevertheless, each child brings something. It is important that teachers determine what skills and knowledge the child has already acquired, identify what each child needs to learn, and plan how best to meet those needs.

Assessing each child's developmental skills can assist the teacher in deciding what and how to teach and when to teach it. In this approach, the teacher is assessing a child's skill development for instructional planning. The assessment does not tell why the child has certain skills already and does not have others, nor does it tell what socioeconomic level or background experiences are brought to the school. An assessment does tell the teacher where the child is now and helps her decide how best to meet the learning needs of each child.

Parent communication. For many parents, especially those who are recent immigrants or refugees, the school is an alien place. In many of the third world countries, education has been reserved for the *elite*, and few children of middle-income and almost none from lower income families are given the opportunity to attend school. Because members of the family may have a long history of non-participation in the school systems, they may have little or no understanding of their roles and responsibilities. Even native parents may often exhibit a great deal of hesitation to become involved in their children's education for a variety of reasons—fear of being perceived as pushy and demanding, lack of time and energy, or feelings of guilt and uncertainty.

For many parents, learning how to work successfully with early childhood teachers will profoundly affect the education of all of their children throughout their schooling. Also, by establishing an open channel of communication with parents, teachers can share important information at an early stage and avoid some of the problems that may arise later.

It falls to the teacher to initiate this communication, and it continues to be a teacher's responsibility until parents feel secure enough to initiate contacts on their own. In some situations the parents may never feel secure enough to take the first step, and the only alternative is for the teacher to continue to take the lead.

Harsh realities. After all of the theories have been expounded and the rhetoric presented, teachers of young children must face the realities of Monday morning. It is extremely helpful for every teacher to have an updated resource guide to the community, which may be available through a local college or agency or assembled and updated by the teachers themselves. Knowledge of community support services, such as food and clothing banks, is helpful in meeting the needs of children who may arrive at school with less than adequate family support at home.

Conclusion

It is important for the early childhood teacher to be aware of and constantly reexamine the assumptions on which her program is based. Outdated or invalid beliefs will result in programs that are not relevant to the needs of the children. Current changes in socioeconomic structures in the United States challenge many previously held assumptions. Teachers must abandon a middle-class orientation toward education, shed stereotyped notions about family structure, and cease making assumptions about a child's learning needs based on the child's background. The design of an early childhood curriculum and the determination of each child's strengths and weaknesses must be based upon a realistic view of contemporary society and an individual assessment of each child.

GAIL RAYMOND is an associate professor in the Department of Educational Psychology at the University of South Carolina in Columbia. She is the author of the Developmental Assessment and Instruction for Success in the Early Years (DAISEY).

DEAN K. MCINTOSH is a retired professor from the Department of Educational Psychology at the University of South Carolina in Columbia.

Children Are Caught—
Between Home and School,
Culture and School

Betsy West

Although diversity of experience and culture is educative, it may also contribute to increased difficulties for a classroom teacher. When the values and habits of the parents differ significantly from those of the school and the teacher, there is unspoken conflict between the two, and the child is caught in that conflict. First, let it be noted that teachers should anticipate such conflicts because most teachers have internalized middle-class mores and customs (whether or not they were actually reared in middle-class homes); yet most of the children in their care are likely not from middle-class homes (see statistics and comments about downward mobility in Raymond & McIntosh article, p. 116).

Second, the conflict may seem keener in schools that serve young children because they have not yet learned to "play the system" as well as older children, to pretend conformance to expectations different from those they are used to. Also, value or cultural conflicts may be more difficult to explain to younger children than to older ones. (If the truth be told, however, few teachers of older children try to explain cultural conflicts; they just demand that the student play by their rules when at school.)

Certainly, many differences in children are individual differences, but some differences arise because the children's subcultures, ethnicity, or family lifestyles are unlike those of the school and the teacher. Understanding those background factors may help teachers preclude problems generated by the differences—or at least find more satisfactory means of coping with those problems.

Individual versus group

In the United States we glorify individualism, and (at least verbally) we also glorify cooperation, without admitting that sometimes those two values are contradictory. Preschool children may come from homes where both values are stressed, but frequently certain ethnic groups stress cooperation and even communal ownership more than middle-class Anglican Americans do. In child care programs teachers expect both individualism and cooperation, but it is often unclear to the child when we expect which.

At home and at school we give children mixed signals about sharing. We may say "Share your toys with your friends," but when a visiting child breaks an expensive toy, it's "I told you you'd have to take care of your toys. . . . Yes, I told you to share, but why did you let him play with *that* toy?" At school we say, "Share the playground equipment," "Take your turn in line" (and we have lots of lines in schools), and "You can both play in the house corner." Still, many of our activities are designed for individual work or play. Even the colorful charts in our classrooms seem to teach competition rather than cooperation. What's stressed here is how many smiling faces are beside one name as compared to someone else's. Children from certain cultural groups have been taught that the group is always more important than the individual and that it is wrong to draw attention to one's self even by an outstanding achievement.

Mine is often one of the first words of middle-class children, but some children never think in terms of "my" crayons, "my" room. They have been taught that ownership is by the group rather than by the individual. At school, then, using or even taking crayons or a pencil from another is not considered stealing. Children from a relatively communal subculture or from extreme poverty, who may share a single coat or pair of shoes with siblings, simply cannot perceive of taking another's lunch in the same way that a middle-class child would perceive it. Yet we, as teachers, sometimes behave as though we believe that children are born understanding the concept of private ownership. When we so carefully give each child his own space or particular supply of materials, are we teaching private ownership or are we teaching selfishness? Indeed, where do we want to draw the line between the two?

Family patterns

One of the differences between a child's perception and that of the teacher may be the concept of family. Recently, during a lull in a show-and-tell group, Karen said something to Kia that prompted her friend to respond, "Ask your daddy." Karen replied, "I ain't got a daddy," but almost immediately grinned and said, "Oh, that's right. I'm going to get a new daddy next week." Kia announced, "Teacher, teacher! Karen's mommy is getting married next week." Karen corrected her: "No, she's not. I just get a new daddy every two or three months."

The teacher, conservative in her lifestyle and beliefs and with only a few years of teaching experience, was flustered by the comment and feared discussion of any controversial issues. She quickly canceled the rest of the show-and-tell time and immediately put the children to work on quiet readiness workbooks. That was much safer.

The teacher's body language and change of attitude must have implied to the child that something was wrong with what happened at her house. Somewhere, sometime, concerned teachers have to let children know that there are different groupings of people called "family"; that love and care are the important elements in a family; and that there are families without fathers, families without mothers, families of two adults of the same gender, and so on. There are various ways to do this in the curriculum and its activities, but the crucial part is for the teacher to be respectful of the differences presented and of the different environments from which children come.

The rate of serial monogamy continues to increase, and there are many reasons to be concerned about that phenomenon—reasons that do indeed affect children. But the child is not in a position to change those trends. We know that the self-concept of young children is largely developed by significant others in their lives. What we as teachers sometimes fail to realize is that we may damage the child's self-concept when we are critical, overtly or covertly, of those who are the significant persons in that child's life.

Sex roles

Even though family patterns and arrangements are changing (more single-parent families, more working parents, and so forth), many American families continue to teach traditional sex roles. Confusion may arise, therefore, when the child enters a child care program where boys are encouraged to cook and dress up and girls are encouraged to play with blocks, trucks, and road equipment. Again, how these differences are handled is more important than the fact that there are differences.

To the boy who says, "My daddy don't want me to play with dolls 'cause that's sissy," we can easily respond, "I bet your father loved you when you were a baby just as he loves you now. Pretending the doll is your baby is really pretending you are a grown man who can be a daddy." And we can casually tell the father what we've said without demanding an attitudinal change on his part.

In an age when more emphasis is rightly put on androgyny, teachers need to remember that gender identification is still a necessary part of the child's maturing process. It is possible that some teachers stress broader, nontraditional roles for boys more than they do for girls. In observing a preschool for an entire semester, I often saw the teacher and aides encourage boys to play in the house corner, to dress up, and to cook, but I didn't see equal encouragement for the girls to become involved in nontraditional roles. When the girls themselves initiated play with *boys' toys*, the teachers protected their rights to take turns, but I did not see the active encouragement of girls to play telephone repair person, ambulance driver, or fire fighter. Indeed, the girls were sometimes given considerable approval (albeit with bemusement) when they dressed up and assumed grown-up (coquettish) styles of walking and other mannerisms. Again, this is an area in which preschool teachers need to look at themselves very carefully. Do we want males to change their roles more than we want females to change theirs? Or is it only that female educators want this more?

Ethnicity

Some of the differences children reflect result from their ethnic or cultural experience. We must be careful not to assume that children of similar racial or ethnic backgrounds are compatible. There are social class differences and personality differences within each ethnic and racial group. We must remember that other countries also have stratification. A child may refer to another from his native land as *just a fisherman* in the same manner that Americans refer to a stereotypical *hillbilly*. We may assume similarities that may not be there. We assume that Asian children should be compatible and helpful to each other or that Blacks should get along with each other. Why? Goodness knows many Whites don't get along with each other. With immigrant children it may be more helpful to ask a child who is a native speaker of English to be the *partner*.

School activities

Sometimes it is the school activities themselves that are the subject of differences with parents. Most early childhood educators at least give lip service to Dewey's concept that one of the purposes of education is to broaden the child's experience, his or her horizons. In trying to achieve that goal, however, we may find ourselves in conflict with the more narrow perceptions of the home environment and in conflict with parents who actually do not want the experiences of their children to include anything that doesn't reinforce the habits and values of home.

All early childhood educators know about the values of water play, finger painting, and other messy activities. The well-known Sexsmith Demonstration Preschool in Vancouver, British Columbia, used such activities in meaningful and educative ways. But some of their students came from traditional Chinese backgrounds. Because schooling was extremely important, the little girls were dressed in their finest clothes to come to school, not the jeans and T-shirts of their Canadian peers. By the end of the day their dresses were frequently splattered with paint.

The primary child care of one Chinese girl lay with a grandmother who was perhaps 60 years old when she had immigrated. This grandmother certainly didn't expect such messiness at school, and she was further confused about why parents were invited to the school so frequently. From her point of view, teachers were the experts and shouldn't have parents telling them what to do. Nonetheless, she tried to meet the educators' expectations and eventually yielded to their urgings to express her feelings. Although her English was minimal, she made her point in no uncertain tone: "School too messy. Water and paint make too much ironing pretty dresses. School learning better from books."

That grandmother did not share the educators' ideas of learning, and she certainly didn't want her grandchild wearing jeans to school, although that seemed to the teachers to be the easiest solution. Note that the first solution they thought of meant that someone else should do the changing or compromising. It is to

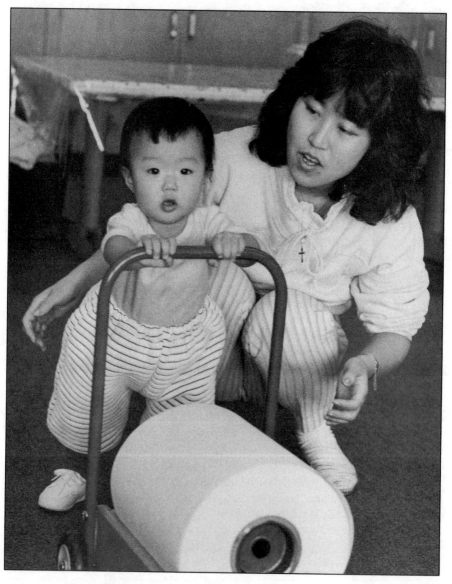

their credit that they caught themselves and offered to send notes home to inform the parents when there would be exceptionally messy activities—and I expect they were more careful to see that children were attired in their aprons.

Language

The language that children hear outside of school often differs from what they hear at school or what the teacher considers appropriate. Early childhood teachers have long noted the variety of euphemisms that children from different backgrounds use for genitalia and excretion. Sometimes they accept the child's usage, sometimes they add their own euphemisms, and sometimes they gradually substitute more scientific labels. In spite of this familiarity with different usage, however, teachers sometimes show their surprise or disdain when the words come up at times other than bathroom breaks.

In a lesson about animals and the sounds they make, the teacher mentioned felines. She referred to a domestic cat as "kitty-cat" and later said "pussy." At that point, however, a student told her, "Hell, Miz Murdock, pussies don't make noise; they're for other things." The fact that few students laughed did not alleviate Ms. Murdock's shock.

If teachers consider levels of usage a necessary concept for children to learn if they are to function in broader segments of society than the one in which they are reared, they do have to explain that some people use different terms and that some terms are considered inappropriate in certain settings. Still this *correction* must be done without putting down the child who uses the terms as he has heard and learned them.

Orderliness

The degree of organization and order varies greatly among families—and also among teachers. Even so, most child care programs and their teachers necessarily have considerable organization of time, space, materials, and activities. If children come from homes where "a place for everything and everything in its place" is the practice, the children respond easily to similar demands in school. But if the child is from a home where there are no toys, it may seem like punishment to have to put away all the toys, including her favorite, even for story hour. Children who live in homes in which belongings are casually piled in disarray may not be able to understand the teacher's *obsession* with order.

The structure of time may be another part of this problem. Middle-class children will have already had considerable experience with their parents keeping schedules and making appointments. They will have been a part of planning for the future and delayed gratification: "Take your nap and we'll go to the park." "Eat your vegetables and you can have dessert." They are likely to be more cooperative as we try to get the classroom decorated before parents' night or some other deadline.

To children who have come from families preoccupied with surviving from day to day, it may seem foolhardy to interrupt current play for some future good (like a party connected with parents' night) that they and their parent(s) may be unable to attend. Such lack of cooperation can be quite disruptive to the goals of the group and annoying to the teacher. In reality, such children simply have not had the socialization for school that some of their middle-class peers have had.

Locale

Children in any kind of preschool or child care live in a more confined space during these hours than do rural children. There are fences around their yards, and implicit in every fence or physical barrier is a notion that someone or something must be kept in or out. Early childhood educators conscientiously take children on walks to explore the neighborhood or the park. But isn't that a euphemism? We may be allowing them to observe—a worthwhile and educative experience. We point out various plants, colors, buildings—but explore? Hardly. We want them to hold the hands of their partners; we don't want them to go in someone's yard (we have to teach the concept of private property); we want to cover the planned route in the allowed time.

A child who had spent his entire five years in a megalopolis recently visited a grandmother whose home is near a small creek in a city. She took him to explore the shoreline, walking through the adjoining yard of neighbors (whom, in fact, she didn't know). But it was the child who kept looking and saying, "This isn't your yard. Will they get us for being here?" There were attitudes to overcome before his curiosity turned to the holes and rocks, plants, color, birds, and mud of the shore.

As a high-rise resident, I watched a father play ball with his son every night—in a space about three feet square that bordered a busy street. It was pleasing to watch their interaction, but I kept thinking of how that experience was developing that child's notion of space. He would probably be like an eight-year-old I know who begs to go to the shopping mall after the stores close: "The mall is a place to run!" There is no place in urban or suburban America for children to run freely. Imagine such a child turned loose in a pasture or field. Even with the best of visuals and children's stories, how can we explain suburban or rural life to a child who has only lived in the inner city of Hong Kong, San Francisco, or Miami?

Not only does locale influence a child's understanding of what space means, it may also affect his awareness of noise and silence. One school in Vancouver took a class on a field trip to a mountain so they could see snow. They were impressed, but more striking was the open space without buildings and the *quiet*. No background noise of traffic or sounds of passersby. The quietness was as new to them as the snow.

Noise level

Children who live in crowded circumstances may have a greater tolerance for background noise than others. But most early childhood teachers want absolute quiet while they give instructions or read a story. We want to teach children that it is rude to speak when someone else is speaking. On the other hand, the children in our classes today have grown up in homes where everyone talks while the television is on, particularly during commercials. Even the polite child may not consider his behavior rude if he isn't drowning out the teacher. Sometimes we're told, "Go ahead with the story, teacher. I'm just talking to Juan." Television keeps on going, why can't teachers?

Tactility and aggression

Early childhood teachers are often surprised at the degree of physicalness of their children. Some teachers complain that certain children *get right up* in their faces. Also, the degree of touching considered common or acceptable varies greatly across ethnic and social class lines. Children from large families may be more used to considerable touching but may resent touching by nonfamily. A teacher who considers a pat on the head or shoulder as a sign of affection may have it shrugged off quite vehemently or even squeamishly. Among some children this preference for nontouching may come from a strong sense of privacy that has been established in their upbringing and, in recent years, may have been intensified by parental reaction to media reports of sexual abuse of children.

Sometimes of greater concern is tactility that is aggressive. Holding, hitting, kicking, and biting may not occur just among peers but may also be directed at the teachers. This violates the middle-class image of respect due authority figures. And the openness and vehemence are contrary to the middle-class ideal of tone modulation and reserve.

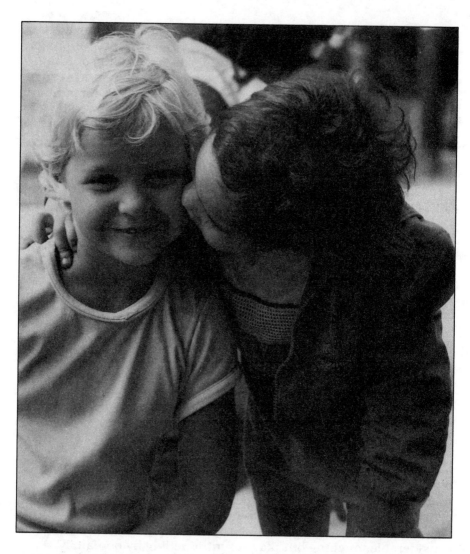

Although we encourage noise and movement on the playground, we expect children to shift to a much quieter and less active mode when they are inside. This pattern of behavior may be a result of personality, but it may also be a result of the child's observations and experience. We should not be surprised that children who may see adults yell and hit each other also behave in this manner. If discussion is not the model children have witnessed, how can we expect them to know how to talk out their problems?

Further, some have been taught to *stand up and fight*: "Only sissies don't fight back." "Stand up for your rights." "Punch his lights out if he calls you that again." And those children are in groups with children who have been told, "It takes two to make a fight" or "Don't hit back; the teacher can settle it." The conflicts arising from these two extremes are further confused by the contradictory messages (verbal and nonverbal, manifest and latent) that we as teachers give through our responses: punishing or shaming (either the aggressor or the victim) or helping each child see the consequence of his or her actions.

The degree of aggression to be tolerated is certainly an area that demands that teachers analyze their own educational philosophies. Do we want to let children see that school rules are different from those at home but just as authoritarian? Do we really want to show reasons for the rules—who made them, why, what would be the consequences of each? To what extent do we want to teach independence and self-reliance? Do we actually want to teach children to be concerned for the welfare of their peers or *to mind their own business*?

Sometimes we teachers criticize strict, authoritarian parents but refuse to see that we are equally dogmatic about the rules of the classroom and school. If we would face the broader ethical questions in these dilemmas instead of substituting one unquestionable authority for another, children would likely have more opportunity to advance through the levels of moral judgment. The tragedy is that the *good* students learn to meet expectations and play their roles in different situations—they learn to conform, not to reason. They learn how to accept discipline, not to self-discipline. Again, the educational setting contributes to the mixed message of society rather than helping children understand the conflicts in human relations.

Peer acceptance

If a child's background is similar to that of the teacher, the teacher may not even realize that understanding the culture is automatically part of the planning and teaching process. When our background is different from those of our students in any of the ways mentioned, it is necessary for us to be consciously aware of those backgrounds so that our planning and teaching processes are equally effective for all. Sometimes the differences are as basic as cleanliness, but have far broader implications.

> What of the unnurtured child? He is the child who comes to school dirty, with unbrushed teeth, smelly ears, filthy hair, and often unfed. The children single him out immediately, and at a very early age he becomes an observer rather than a participant in life. Social services is usually uninterested and unable to help this kind of child and is reluctant to become involved unless there is extreme neglect or abuse. I have found working with these parents has some positive effect, which usually lasts about one week, until the lifestyle

patterns fall back in place. How does a child from this kind of home ever grow in self-esteem? Aside from patching (grooming at school, etc.), how can a professional be of help? I have watched these children remain outcasts—always on the edge of things, wishing, throughout their school years, and have found my own ability to help inadequate. (Diane Burger, kindergarten teacher at The Mountain School, Sun Valley, Idaho)

It's easy to feel that anyone can keep his or her children clean, but we must stop to think of how much soap and laundromats cost. And we forget that water is often shut off because of unpaid utilities. Realistically, teachers must admit that, short of adopting the individual child, they cannot solve all of the social problems that affect children. But within the confines of the time and space we share with that child, we can arrange circumstances that provide opportunity for her participation and success. The hair may be stringy and the clothes dirty, but we can compliment the smile. We can do something about her self-concept, at least at school. And, gradually, the child can assume some responsibility for her own cleanliness.

The more difficult task is encouraging the other children to include them. We can demonstrate that we aren't afraid of getting close to the child: "I want to sit beside Emily today." We can choose that child as leader when they play follow-the-leader. We all know that children can be unkind and alarmingly candid in expressing their distaste, but a part of our job as teachers is to teach them to respect others, beginning in our classrooms. We can *guide* the reactions of the other children.

Conclusion

Some differences between schools and home are unavoidable. It is not so much the differences themselves that are troublesome, but rather how the school personnel handle those differences. We can be understanding without agreeing. If we, as teachers, establish rapport with the children and their parents, if we earn the respect of the parents, if it is clear to children and parents that we care about them, if we take the time to explain our reasons for activities, if we give parents an opportunity to explain their points of view—if we do all of those things, not just one or two, in most cases the parents will accept the policies and practices of the school.

At the height of the civil rights demonstrations, a parent said to me, "You and me ain't never going to agree about niggers, Mrs. West. But I do know that you love my boy, so you won't teach him nothing that will hurt him." Having already established positive relations with the child and his parents, I could then explain that their son was growing up in a world that would be different from the world they had known, and that the school was trying to prepare him to function in that world.

In the most extreme cases, it may become necessary to say that while parents have the right to teach their values to their children, the school has the obligation to prepare children to function in a broader society. That may give the parents the responsibility for improving their teaching so that the child is presented two strong influences that educate him. The teacher might point out that she never tells the child that the parents are wrong, and it would be easier for the child if the parents didn't openly say that the teacher is wrong.

For a few parents such a disagreement eventually may mean withdrawing their child from the school. Neither the school nor the individual teacher should abrogate their responsibility to the larger society nor to the task of preparing the child to function in the larger society. If we make the extra effort, in most cases we can find the communication skills to persuade or, at the very least, differ without being arrogant or disagreeable. Perhaps, sadly, we teachers are most dogmatic when we have weak points or secretly feel that the parents aren't worth our time. I doubt that teachers can really love children if they hold the parents in contempt. If children are products of their experiences, so too are parents. And they likewise deserve respect and understanding.

At the time of this book's original publication, BETSY WEST taught social foundations of education and multicultural education at Wichita State University, Wichita, Kansas. She spent a sabbatical in Vancouver, observing the Sexsmith ESL Demonstration Preschool of the Child Study Centre at the University of British Columbia.

Diversity and Conflict: The Whole World Will Never Sing in Perfect Harmony

Jim Greenman

Can there be diversity without conflict? I doubt it. Woodstock nation never came to pass. Little creatures of the forest haven't come together. We don't have many models of diversity functioning without conflict. The Cosby show isn't real; that life doesn't exist in very many places.

We don't like diversity in this country, but we like to believe that we do. We pretend a lot. We pretend that we don't have social classes. We pretend that racism is something of the past. We don't really want group homes for retarded people in our neighborhoods—or even group homes for adults with physical handicaps. Most religions are broken up into a lot of splinter groups. Even roommates don't get along well if they are too different.

Diversity, like many things that are good for us, usually isn't comfortable. The problem is not just in a failure to communicate or in ignorance, the common and convenient characterizations of the problem.

Child development stories

I was watching a little boy in a program in Chinatown who was about to conduct an experiment in the water table—"Can gerbils swim?", a follow-up to his dramatic investigation—"Can gerbils fly?" A very patient teacher, at the end of her rope (not unlike the unfortunate gerbil), said, "If you do that, we are going to have to tell your grandfather." When I asked several early child educators what they thought of the story, there was agreement that this was bad child development. But why is it bad child development in a culture where disgracing your family actually means something, where grandfathers are important, where children have genuine respect for their grandfathers? Why is that bad child development to bring in the family context?

Another story . . . . There was a wonderful man working with babies in an infant program. While very gentle and quiet, one of the things he did a good deal of was active physical interaction with the babies, which they loved. He was cautioned that this was bad child development. Well, is it? Is the male caregiving style, which often is much more physically stimulating and less soothing than most female caregiving styles, bad child development? Or is it just different? Is the fussy caregiving of a 68-year-old woman (or man) of various ethnicity bad child development?

Another story . . . . Visiting a child care program in the Arctic, I watched a five-year-old Eskimo boy working with an 80-year-old man. They messed about with a motor for 45 minutes. The silence was deafening; hardly a word was exchanged, but the unspoken communication between the old man and the boy was incredible. Forty-five minutes with no words spoken—was that bad child development?

There has been an influx of Hmong people from Laos and Cambodia to Minnesota. A child care center with many Hmong children was trying to improve the infant and toddler program by hiring more Hmong staff. The center believed, as I do, in a language-rich environment and much personal one-to-one interaction between caregiver and baby. With Hmong staff, they got very little language and very little interaction with toddlers. Bad child development?

What would be normal in Hmong society? Mothers strap their babies to them, and this happened at the center. They have constant bodily interaction, but not the interaction we know. Toddlers are often the responsibility of older children, not just the mother. In the Hmong world, once a child stops nursing—when the mother turns her attention to the new baby—the older baby begins to be cared for by the four-year-old or the seven-year-old or the other older children.

It was hard for the Hmong caregivers to suddenly relate to children in a new way—our way, a way in which children are divided into tight age groups and children have no responsibility for caring for siblings (often or ever!). A Hmong child care center would be organized very differently.

Diversity on the job

What is good work behavior? Nearly all directors would argue that being on time is essential to good work behavior. If you are not on time, you are a real pain to many. It's hard to conceive of people who are not on time as responsible or good workers.

I worked with a very talented teacher, a young Indian man who had one problem—he was rarely on time. There are all sorts of jokes about minorities and their sense of time—CP (colored people) time, Indian time. There is always some truth behind the usually derogatory joke. Cultures have different sets of time, and the importance of "on time" varies. You only "miss the boat" if the boat leaves on a tight schedule. An alternative—the time the boat leaves is when everyone is there. In this case, the teacher also had public transportation to deal with—during Minnesota winters. No matter, his lateness was usually viewed as a character flaw. Staff who are often late fall prey to our cultural stereotypes—they are lazy, disorganized, or can't get it together.

But we (speaking for American middle-class White people, I guess) are very strange about time. If I—the director—was late, people assumed it was because I was so busy. We are willing to grant dispensation for some people because we assume that their lateness occurred because of factors beyond their control, socially redeeming factors at that. Not incidentally, many of these people are of higher status or social class and in more powerful positions.

Interestingly, it is usually acceptable for these individuals to keep those lesser souls waiting, perhaps even for the supervisory conference to lecture on the importance of on-time behavior.

Another situation will come up in how the work is divided. Many of our models of good infant care include adults who are on the floor with kids. There are cultural and age differences here, and a lot of people aren't going to feel comfortable rolling on the floor with babies. If our model of good infant care is that everyone has to be on the floor with babies, we are not going to be able to tolerate as much diversity.

Diversity without conflict?

No room for diversity. Where in the midst of diversity is there less conflict? One place is where there is no tolerance for any diversity in thought or behavior, where diversity really doesn't matter. You're not going to get much conflict from diversity on an assembly line. If there are clear behavioral prescriptions, diversity isn't an issue. Many child care centers manage this way. Everything is prescribed, routines are clear, and it works smoothly. Make it routine, and issues—however important—are less likely to come up.

Room for diversity. Allowing room for diversity is another and more preferable way to reduce conflict. If there is room for territories and there are clear boundaries, then individuals can do their job their way. Public schools are often an example of this. The right of the teacher to close her door and do her own thing makes public schools, given the right administration, places where very talented, diverse individuals flourish side by side. The doors are closed. No one is going to see it. Yet room only makes a difference if there is enough autonomy so I can be myself in my space.

Diversity also requires times and places to retreat. A Black teacher I worked with periodically would say, "I've just got to find a place where I can get away from White people." I understood entirely because as one of the one or two males around (usually), I needed the same thing—I needed to get away from women. For women who work in all-male environments, the feeling is the same. We need to get away; we need to be with people that we feel we can be ourselves with.

Sufficient numbers. Another thing that supports diversity is sufficient numbers. I was director of a center for a long time that always had a lot of men, and I'm convinced that one of the reasons is that we crossed the critical threshold of numbers. There were three men, so it was much more comfortable for men to work there. Once you have more than one or two of any given minority—

age, gender, race—the organization is under more pressure to accommodate. Numbers count.

Beyond coping: Valuing diversity

There are places, but not many, where diversity really works and greatly enriches the organization. Based on appreciation and understanding grounded in respect, these child care centers have a basic belief that good care and education comes in different forms—that what is good care is allowed to be arguable. There is a high tolerance for difference. In most organizations, the earnest proclamation of valuing differences is instantly contradicted by talking to those who are different.

For a person or a program, the key to understanding and respecting differences is having a good sense of who you are and knowing the boundaries of what you are. Not too many child care programs are that self-aware, and there is a reason for this. In child care, you have no time to talk, so you really don't talk about things that may lead to controversy. You don't thrash out exactly what you are, what you believe. What are the boundaries of how much language you need to have in your program? If you really believe that classrooms have to be incredibly verbal, it's going to limit the kind of cultures you have in that classroom. If you believe that all children process information the same way or use the same social behavior, it's the same thing. Knowing who you are, being comfortable with that, and knowing the boundaries of your ideology and the program will reduce conflict.

What becomes a staff issue when you have diversity? The same things that become an issue when you don't have diversity. Who is in charge here? How can this person tell me what to do? What am I supposed to do, as opposed to this other person? A program that is going to have a diverse staff or treat parents with respect has to articulate what they expect from staff and parents. If they don't, there will be conflict with racial, ethnic, or gender overtones.

Good programs have to solve problems. They have or make the time and energy to do it. They discuss social issues and they discuss the issues that come from diversity. I worked in a center that believed that children should get dirty and be little scientists—it had a wonderful adventure playground. Parents, particularly Black parents, would say "We don't want our kids going outside. We spend an hour and a half on their hair. Two minutes later they are covered with sand. We can't get that stuff out, and we spend our whole evening cleaning it up. So we don't want our kids going outside." For awhile, our earnest and empathic response was "Gee, that is too bad. But this really is good for the children."

Of course, our knowing response implied, "You poor, ignorant person, valuing appearance over good child development." Conflict continued and we learned. Now the response to these sorts of issues is, "Okay, let's figure this out. Obviously it's important to you how your child looks. And you know it's very good for these children to have these sorts of experiences. Let's come up with a solution." The assumption is two legitimate points of view—let's work it out together. In this instance, the answer was shower caps for the children.

The sad reality is that all that many programs have time for is often the doing—not thinking, problem solving, and growing. If things are going well, it means smoothly, comfortably—which means that the gerbil doesn't die dramatically after all and people do not fight. But it doesn't mean that children are not getting less than they deserve, that some are not lost in the cracks, that cultures are not being devalued and diminished, and that we are not losing all the wonderful ways that people are different.

Diversity is the spice of life. It also makes us sneeze a lot. If we believe in diversity, we have to take the time to think it through for our programs.

JIM GREENMAN is a child care consultant from Minneapolis, Minnesota, and director of programs and facilities for Resources for Child Care Management.

Meeting the Needs of All Children— An Indian Perspective

Harold GossMan

Challenge stereotypes. Look at the curriculum materials that you're using in your classrooms. Look for accuracies and inaccuracies. Find out what Indian life is like today. Present this picture to children.

My nephew's daughter is now five years old and attends pre-school. She came home and told her family that she had learned a new song at school. Her father was very proud of the accomplishment, and when I went to visit, she was asked to sing the new song for her uncle. The song was "Old MacDonald." She began to sing, "Old MacDonald had a farm. . . ." She paused and thought for a minute trying to remember the words. She began again; still she couldn't remember and had difficulty with the words at the end of the phrase. She thought for a moment more, than began again, this time with the look and sound of confidence. She sang loudly, "Old MacDonald had a farm, hey ya, hey ya, ho."

My grandfather was born in 1889 on the southern Cheyenne reservation. He came out of the tipi and was educated through the boarding school system. It wasn't because he wanted to, it was because he was taken to the school. His clothes were changed, his hair was cut, his lifestyle and his values were changed. Indians have been the victims of forced assimilation. Other minorities have had to deal with forced segregation. Our culture has been taken away and replaced by a melting pot culture that we didn't ask for. I was raised by my grandparents in western Oklahoma, on what was originally the southern Cheyenne and Arapaho reservation.

As with most children, I didn't realize at the time how the attitudes of the community around me were affecting me. I don't think now that we, as adults, realize how our attitudes and actions in general affect the children that we work with. The two most important things we can do for children are (1) to instill a sense of worth as we teach, and (2) to realize that everything we do, consciously and unconsciously, impacts on this sense of worth. Thoughtless words and subtle actions can quickly undermine our program objectives.

As an adult, I feel that I'm expected to be toughened to the kinds of things that people say inadvertently. While working at a small community college in Oklahoma, I was asked to participate in a Thanksgiving dinner program—we were to have the faculty and staff serve the students who didn't go home for the holidays. When I came into the cafeteria to do my part, the vice president of the college looked around and acknowledged my presence with the statement, "Our Thanksgiving is now complete; our Indian is here."

She's not an insensitive or uncaring woman; she is educated and intelligent. But the fact remains that the statement was thoughtless. I know how those words affected me as an adult—they brought about a feeling that I was the token. How do such words and attitudes affect children? Whenever we talk about any child and about any child's culture, heritage, or ancestry, our words are affecting that child's sense of worth.

Of course, Thanksgiving is the one time of the year when Indians are quite visible. One summer when I was in school I received a contract with the community arts and humanities council to

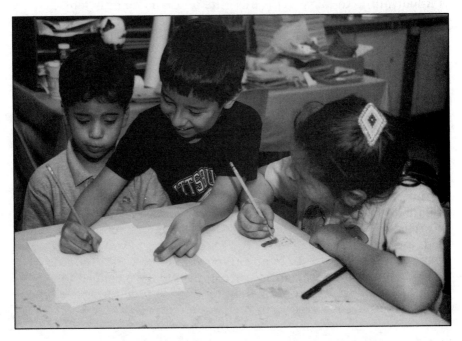

prepare cultural presentations, to talk about Indians. I thought, "This is going to be great."

September came and, just as school was starting, I got a few engagements. In October the number of requests picked up. During November I was busy every day, going to a school or a civic group meeting. Then came December and January; the presentations were not in demand—nobody wanted to hear about Indians in January. But for Thanksgiving, the work was plentiful, the presentations were popular, and I was really busy. Is this the only image of Indian culture that we want to give children?

How can you help? By recognizing and increasing awareness of how other people regard themselves. Some people look for labels. I am sometimes asked, "Are you Indians? Native Americans? What do you prefer to be called?" We weren't Indians before Christopher Columbus discovered us. Native Americans? Well, we were here before there was an America. We are aboriginal, but that doesn't sound very good to me, and the Australians have a lock on that.

To affix a label on anyone, we first have to look to the context of the categories. By race, I am an American Indian; by citizenship, I am an American citizen. (I have also been told that by treaty with the Sioux nations and Canada, I'm also a Canadian citizen.) By nationality, I am an enrolled member of the Oglala Sioux nation. I am also a hereditary member of the Cheyenne and Arapaho nations in Oklahoma. I am a resident of Oklahoma. So I am all of these things.

What label is affixed to people is not what is of importance. What is important is to move away from the tendency to only look at history. We don't look at where Indians come from in terms of geography or society, but we look at them in terms of history.

Indian children, like all children, are trying to figure out who they are and what their place is in society. If we give children inaccuracies about any culture, we do them a disservice. If we give Indian children inaccuracies about their own culture, we cause irreparable harm.

I will acknowledge that it is extremely difficult to find good resource materials on Indian culture. And it is equally as difficult to find people who agree on the value of any particular resource. There are items that we can identify in resource materials and raise awareness of the context in which they are presented.

I find items in many books that relate to Indians—American Indians were great hunters, Indians were skilled craftsmen, Indians used whatever they could find that was edible as a source of food, Indians were great warriors. Taken at literal value, such resources would indicate to an unknowing reader that Indians don't exist anymore, the entire race of people have ceased to exist, there are no more Indians. Everything and everyone in these types of references are referred to in the past tense.

Usually when Indian culture is referenced, it is looked at from a historical perspective. When we exclusively use these kinds of resources, we are telling Indian children that they have to put their culture aside because it's a dead culture, it's behind us, it's historical, it only exists in memory. And the message that children receive is that either they don't exist or their racial and cultural identity as Indians is not important.

In order to provide a more realistic portrayal of Indians in today's world, talk to Indians. Pick up a phone book. Look under "Indian," "Native American," or "American Indian." There is a Native American center in almost every major metropolitan area in the country—Boston, Cleveland, Dallas, Minneapolis, and Los Angeles are just a few. These centers are where people group together to talk about the things of everyday life. Contact the Department of Education, Offices of Indian Education, in Washington, D.C., and in most states. There are Title IV Indian education projects in the public schools. There are 105 Indian Head Start programs. There are more than 400 tribal government offices. The people in these offices and programs are willing to share resources and information about their culture.

We don't hear much about Indians as they are today, in everyday life. Our society is telling Indian children that they have to give up being Indian to be successful. Pick up newspapers, textbooks, or resource materials, and try to find out who was the first Indian to participate in professional sports or the first Indian to be elected to public office.

Much of what children do see about Indian culture has some negative connotations for them. Indians are used as mascots (such as the Washington Redskins and the Cleveland Indians). Do you think we will ever hear of the Kansas City Caucasians, Boston Black Guys, or the Washington White Men?

I think, and hope, that the people who named those sports teams probably had good intentions, that they thought they were honoring the people that participated and excelled in their accomplishments for those teams. The Cleveland Indians were named in honor of Alex Sockalexis, a member of the Penobscot Tribe. He was as important to the game of baseball in the 1890s as Babe Ruth, Hank Aaron, and Johnny Bench were in their time, but we lost sight of that. Like everyone else, Indian children need heroes—people like themselves that they can look to as role models.

Now we're looking at how we're going to retain our culture. But keep in mind that *it is not a remnant of a past culture that we are attempting to save, it is a present-day, evolving culture based on very sound values. Today, Indians group together; they practice their beliefs and their culture, and they adhere to traditional values and their religions. They do it in private. They do it at home. They mesh traditional values with contemporary settings.*

In the traditional cultures, Indian children are taught behaviors that may work against them in the classroom. We are somewhat of an invisible population; we just go along and stay in the background. Children are taught to stay back, be quiet, listen, and figure out what's going on. Only speak when you have something to say. As a show of respect, children are taught not to challenge their elders by looking them directly in the eyes or speaking out and questioning what is being taught. But whenever that happens with the Indian children in a classroom setting, we tend to confuse them by contradicting what their families have taught them. We don't bring them out in understanding ways; we don't implement the things that will build their self-concept, that will build their self-image, the things that they can be proud of.

An Indian tradition is to use what is here. As you begin to talk about geography and the names of cities and rivers and streets and towns, you can hardly go through a day without speaking some words that came from one of the Indian languages. Many of the places have Indian names. When we talk about food, it is interesting to note that the pre-Columbian northern European diet consisted mainly of meat and grains. But when northern Europeans came to this continent, they found foods like the Irish potato, Boston baked beans, tomatoes, corn, squash, and all of those wonderful vegetables that we enjoy.

When I give cultural presentations to small children, and sometimes to adults, they ask questions like, "Where do Indians get their food?" I usually tell them Safeway. They ask, "Do you live in a tipi?" I say only in the summer when I go to powwows. Some children are actually frightened when they hear that an Indian is coming to visit! We need to correct misconceptions. We need to look at Indians in the context of today's society and consider some of the contributions that Indians make today.

What I said at the beginning of this chapter was simple, but *so* important: Challenge stereotypes. Look at the curriculum materials that you're using in your classrooms. Look for accuracies and inaccuracies. Find out what Indian life is like today. Present this picture to children.

For further reading

Billman, J. The Native American curriculum: Attempting alternatives to tepees and headbands. *Young Children,* 47(6), 22–25. 1992.

Brady, P. Columbus and the quincentennial myths: Another side of the story. *Young Children,* 47(6), 4–14. 1992.

Greenberg, P. Ideas that work with young children. Teaching about Native Americans? Or teaching about people, including Native Americans? *Young Children,* 47(6), 27–30, 79–80. 1992.

Little Soldier, L. Working with Native American children. *Young Children,* 47(6), 15–21. 1992.

HAROLD GOSSMAN is an enrolled member of the Oglala Sioux Tribe of Pine Ridge, South Dakota, and a hereditary descendent of Cheyenne Chief Roman Nose. He was educated in the boarding school system and attended Louisiana State University and Langston University in Oklahoma. Harold is employed by Three Feathers Associates, the Indian Head Start Resource Center based in Norman, Oklahoma. He provides training and technical assistance in the areas of social service and parent involvement and Indian child welfare to 105 Indian Head Start programs.

All Children Are Special

Jan Cole Krick

At any given time any child can be a child with special needs, and surely any of us who are parents would agree that at certain times we are parents with special needs.

In early childhood programs we often say that all children are special. However, do we really treat all children as if they are special and unique? Not usually. Have we done so historically? No, we haven't. Just look at most public schools, in which conformity is valued more than being different. In early childhood programs we have a chance to treat children as if they are unique and special because we value free choice and expression and because our caregiving relationships with children allow for the development of an intimate bond between adults and children.

But the reality still is that when we talk about children with special needs, we are often talking about the children that are driving us nuts. We are talking about the children who don't conform to our programs, the children who present new challenges.

In order to meet the needs of all children and to keep our programs healthy, we must expand our definition of children with special needs to include any child who has needs beyond those provided in the regular programmed day—for example, Francis, a baby who is fussy with new teeth coming in, or Mary, a preschooler whose baby sister died two hours after birth. Many a child could be a child with special needs at a given point in time, and every child has periods of special need.

In order to meet all of these needs, we must individualize our programs. Programs that present a learning environment to fit multiple levels of development, that allow for leisurely time spent in caregiving routines, and that build respectful relationships with parents benefit normal children as much as they benefit children who have special needs.

Without individualization I have images of assembly-line diapering, children sitting for long periods of time, children standing in lines. These routines are dangerous because they affect the personal relationship that we need to establish with children in order to care for them in a high-quality manner.

Are we going to jeopardize the individual relationship that we must have with children—the very thing that we have to truly make children feel as if they are unique and special?

Why do we serve children with special needs?

Specialized needs and times of special need are part of childhood life. In the population of children in a program, there are children who have specialized needs. These range from the child with fetal alcohol syndrome to the toddler who bites.

We also serve children with special needs because we want to support parents. We want to encourage children's growth and development so that parents see that their children can learn and that there is a future for their children—these children who may be different.

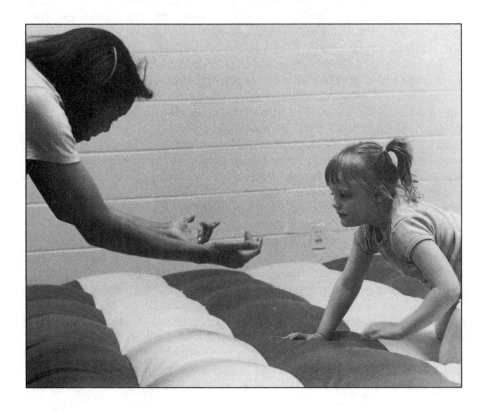

We serve children with special needs because we know that early intervention works. Consider five-year-old Deanna, born to a life with fetal alcohol syndrome. Enrolled in an infant child care program at nine months, she could barely hold up her head.

Although her mother continued to be an alcoholic, the program worked with teenage sisters to improve her nutrition, get her to doctor appointments, bring her to child care every day, and keep track of her medication and other details critical for growth and development. At age five she entered a normal kindergarten. For Deanna, early intervention worked; society benefits.

We serve children with special needs so that our children will (it is hoped) grow up relating to people who are different and so that being different is valued as much as is being the same. We have to broaden our definition of special needs to include all children.

We serve children with special needs because, with some exceptions, it is the law.

We need to create an awareness of special needs—an awareness that makes us sensitive to individual children on an ongoing basis in our programs. Let me share the story of one three-and-a-half-year-old child with special needs. Mandy's day begins at 5:30 A.M.; she is dropped off at child care at 6:30. Four mornings a week she goes to the public school special education preschool, then back to the center to be picked up and taken home.

How many of us could tolerate a schedule like that? The child care staff reported that Mandy frequently fell asleep into her plate of food, and they would try to wake her up to eat before putting her on the afternoon bus. Staff at the therapeutic programs complained that Mandy's mother was overly protective, uncooperative, and difficult to communicate with. In contrast, the child care staff saw her as a protective mother and supported her concerns. A trusted child care teacher often heard her mother say, "She's only three—too little to be on a school bus all day."

At a parent conference Mandy's mother asserted herself and pulled her child out of both therapeutic programs and, with the help of her family, arranged care. After nine months Mandy's mother permitted special programming to begin again, but only after a reasonable schedule was worked out.

Mandy stopped falling asleep in her mashed potatoes, stopped hitting other children, and started to play with them. My point is that Mandy's mother, in her wisdom, recognized the need for protection and Mandy's right to have safe and relaxed days. Perhaps Mandy fell a little more behind temporarily, but in the end she gained a lot in the quality of her life. Mandy was no longer seen as the problem child but as a child with potential for growth.

Mandy had suffered from not fitting into the programming, but it was the programming that was causing the problem.

What happens if we ignore special needs?

We can't dodge these children. They aren't going to go away. If we don't pay attention to their special needs, some will create chaos in our programs. They tear toys off the shelves, run away, and hurt themselves and others. Some children may get lost. Sometimes children *literally* fall through the cracks. It's not enough to see the individual needs of children; we have to be able to get to those needs and meet them. If not, the behavior of some children will disrupt all of the other children, and *none* of the children will have optimal opportunities for development and learning.

The increasing stress in our society may increase the numbers of children who are highly at risk. Without effective intervention, many of these children will be added to the statistics of what is being called the underclass. If we don't serve children with special needs, the quality of our programs will actually go down. Only by paying attention to their individual needs can we successfully provide high-quality care in our programs.

It is important to note that individualizing care and education not only benefits the child who has special needs but also benefits the child who is progressing normally. If we don't bend our programs to meet individual needs, children who are ahead may become our children with special needs. And if we try to treat children as if they are all the same, if we don't pay attention to children's special needs, many of our staff will burn out. When the focus is on sameness or on routines, teachers may simply go through the routines whether they make sense or not.

Ignoring children with special needs can lead to parent dissatisfaction with our programs. Parents whose children get hit or bitten expect us to deal with the problem so that their children are safe. Consider also the parent of the not-so-well child who wants her child kept inside for the day and is told, "I'm sorry, we can't do that here." Or consider the parent of the biting child who is told, "I'm sorry, you can't come back here anymore." Being able to meet children's individual needs will make parents feel more secure and satisfied with the program.

Who are these parents in our programs? Well, sometimes they are low-income families, sometimes they may be families who are having a crisis, sometimes they may be two-parent families who have two full-time jobs and whose life is so busy that they have little time for quality family life. Some parents may have dysfunctional families or be exhausted from the burden of caring for a child with a handicap. The point is that parents are often leading stressful and hectic lives. It is our job to provide them with secure and healthy care for their children and to make sure that their

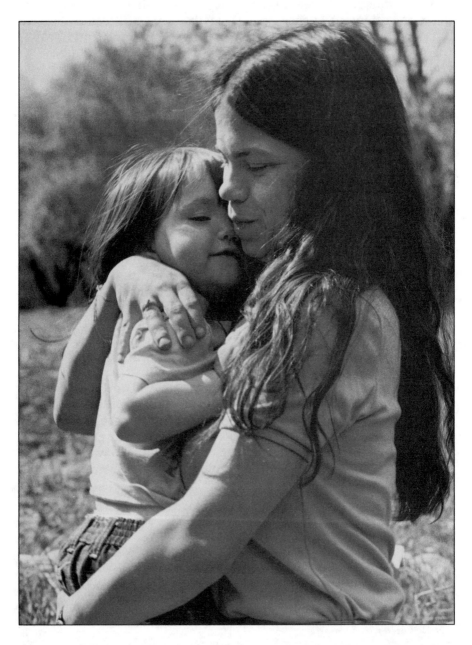

child's experience with us allows parents to see their child as a source of family pleasure.

What do we have to offer children with special needs?

Let me tell you about Rhonda, who came into my classroom 14 years ago. She had witnessed her father shot to death and had experienced a great deal of neglect and abuse. Relatives who cared for her kept her locked in an attic and left food for her on a plate. When her grandmother assumed care for her and brought her to us, she was a ferocious child who wildly destroyed anything or anyone in her way.

Her grandmother enrolled her one day at naptime. She literally destroyed my classroom. She raked all the toys off the shelves, got in my desk and threw markers all over, woke up all of the children who were sleeping—it was sheer chaos. She had a desperate need for love and attention, but everything that she did alienated her from others.

The only goal I had for Rhonda was to make it possible for her to accept love and to calm down enough to learn. Every day for the next year and a half I rocked Rhonda in my arms at naptime. I tried to fill her with all the love and care that she never got. Success with Rhonda was limited, but she eventually adjusted to classroom rules and expectations. After kindergarten I lost track of her.

What did I learn from Rhonda? I learned the value of spending time rocking and soothing a desperate child when she is upset. I learned ways of calming a wild child. I learned that it may be part of my job as a caregiver who believes in individualizing to bathe a child and fix hair attractively. And I learned how to set up a learning environment that was appropriate for *all* of the children in my classroom, even a child as difficult as Rhonda.

I learned how to talk to her grandmother, and I learned how to use community resources when I knew that my classroom did not provide enough support. A church donated money for Rhonda's swimming lessons, a neighbor volunteered to take her to doctor appointments, the Foster Grandparent Program provided the extra hands I needed in my classroom, and the public schools accepted her into a summer school program to give her an "extra boost" before kindergarten.

I learned to have just that extra bit of patience that it takes when I thought I didn't have any left. But most of all I learned to love this child for who she was at that moment, not for what I wanted her to be and not for who she was going to be in the future.

"Special needs" are not things that are exclusive to certain segments of people. By serving the child with obvious special needs as well as the child who has a special need at this time, we serve all children better. We offer safety, acceptance, and pride in their accomplishments. We offer parent support and developmentally appropriate environments. And we offer hope and a future to all of the children that we serve, even where no hope may have existed before.

JAN COLE KRICK is a child care consultant in Minneapolis. She is a former child care director, coordinator of an inner city child care consortium, and an experienced advocate for low-income parents and for children and families with special needs.

Chapter 6
CONSIDERING OUR RESOURCES

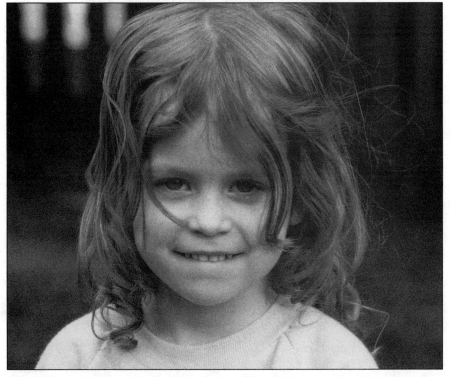

Has "the writer gone beyond and behind the stereotypes, myths, and ideas . . . to develop characters whose ethnic, social, cultural, and personal experiences mesh in all the complex ways they do in real life . . ."?

—Judith Thompson and Floria Woodard
in the *Wilson Library Bulletin*
December 1969

What Are We Really Saying to Children? Criteria for the Selection of Books and Materials

Bonnie Neugebauer

Children receive messages from myriad sources within the context of the early childhood environment. We must be conscious of the messages that come through our words and actions and silences, and we must evaluate the messages inherent in the materials we provide. Only when we are deliberately selecting and evaluating can we hope that the messages children receive while in our care are consistent with the philosophy and goals of our programs. (For a quick, easy way to evaluate your entire library or classroom, ask parents and other staff each to take a few books or other materials and an equal number of photocopies of this checklist to review on their own.)

Look for the messages in children's books

Evaluate the characters

Yes   No

☐   ☐   Do the characters in the story have personalities like real people?

☐   ☐   Do they seem authentic in the way they act and react?

☐   ☐   Do they speak in a style and language that fits their situation?

Yes	No	
☐	☐	Are they real people with strengths and weaknesses rather than stereotypes?
☐	☐	Are characters allowed to learn and grow?
☐	☐	Is their lifestyle represented fairly and respectfully?

Evaluate the situation

☐	☐	Do the characters have power over their own lives?
☐	☐	Do they resolve their own problems and reap their own rewards?
☐	☐	Are human qualities emphasized?

Evaluate the illustrations

☐	☐	Do the illustrations respectfully depict ethnic, age, cultural, economic, ability, and sexual differences? (Illustrations can be humorous, but they must fit the context of the story line and be consistent in portrayal.)
☐	☐	Do the illustrations and the text work well together to communicate the story?
☐	☐	Is the style of illustration appropriate to the story?

Evaluate the messages

☐	☐	Do the messages conveyed, both directly and indirectly, respectfully and accurately portray the human condition?
☐	☐	Are there hidden messages that are demeaning in any way or that reinforce stereotypes?

Evaluate the author/illustrator's credibility

☐	☐	Does the author/illustrator's background and training prepare her or him to present this story? (Do not disregard, but do consider carefully, stories about women written by men, stories about people with handicaps written by people without handicaps, and stories about one ethnic group written by another.)

Consider your selections as a whole

It is not possible for any one book to portray all that we want to say to children, so it is important to look at your whole library:

Yes　No

☐　☐ Are there stories about the contemporary life of a given ethnic group, as well as tales and legends?

☐　☐ Do the cultures represented in your library at least cover (and, optimally, extend well beyond) those cultures represented by the families in your program?

☐　☐ Are there books in which the disability or racial or economic difference is just part of the context for a story about people's lives, as well as books that focus on that particular difference?

Look for the messages in materials and equipment

☐　☐ Does this toy stereotype people by sex, race, age, family situation, physical skills, or intellectual skills?

☐　☐ Does the selection of materials as a whole represent the diversity of humankind?

☐　☐ How long will this toy hold a child's interest?

☐　☐ Can the toy be adapted or used in different ways to change with different interests and ages of children?

☐　☐ Can the toy be combined with other play materials to extend its possibilities?

☐　☐ Is the toy safe, sturdy, and appealing?

☐　☐ Does the packaging of the toy reflect diversity? (If not, throw it away or use it for discussion, and write to the manufacturer.)

☐　☐ Is the way in which children play with these materials consistent with your program's philosophy and goals?

Portions of these criteria were adapted from Beginning Equal: A Manual About Nonsexist Childrearing for Infants and Toddlers *(New York: Women's Action Alliance, Inc. and Pre-School Association, Inc., 1983) and* 10 Quick Ways to Analyze Books for Racism and Sexism, *Council on Interracial Books for Children (Volume 5, Number 3, 1974).*

Reflecting Diversity— Books To Read With Young Children*

Bonnie Neugebauer

Books and catalogs spill off the shelves, over my desk, and onto the floor. The topic we've chosen for this volume is so broad—there are so many pieces, so many ways that we can look at ourselves and others. Where do I begin to sort out the good from the bad, the enriching from the limiting? And even though I began the search for every book that includes through story or illustration ways in which we differ from each other, the gems that I am now searching for are those books that present people as people, including differences as a natural part of life, books that celebrate our humanity.

The ideal of this process would include an even distribution that in itself would reflect the spectrum, but as I worked and read, I realized that to even the distribution, I would have to make too many compromises. The following list is lopsided, with some holes and gaps, but the books it contains meet our criteria and represent what books for young children should be.

1. First of all, they are good stories. They are interesting both to read and to listen to.

2. The illustrations work with the text and in many, many instances are wonderfully delightful or breathtaking.

3. They meet the criteria for book selection set forth on pp. 160–162.

Illustrators, authors, and publishing companies have a long way to go to meet the needs of our children for wonderful stories that

---

*Books described as out of print may still be available from a library. Letters to the publisher requesting reprinting are helpful in letting publishers know that some of us want—and will buy—these little-known but valuable books.

include children of all ethnic groups, all religious groups, all economic situations, and all ability levels playing, living, working, and solving problems together, and discovering their world and their individual and shared humanity.

So in your reading, if you discover a great story about a Jewish child in the midst of a sibling rivalry, a Hmong child using his art to sort out his life, an illustrator who includes handicapped people in her illustrations, remember that name! You have discovered a person who is trying to make a difference; spread the word!

Most of these books are equally useful in living and working with preschool, kindergarten, and primary grade children.

Books rich in diversity

Ada, Alma F. *Abecedario de los animales.* Madrid, Spain: Espasa Calpe, 1990.
Through lively poems and delightful pastel illustrations, children are exposed to the Spanish alphabet.

Ancona, George. *Helping Out.* New York: Clarion, 1985.
People of different ages can share a task and grow closer in the process. Photographs highlight diversity.

Andrews, Jan. *Very Last First Time* (illustrated by Ian Wallace). New York: Atheneum, 1986.
Eva is filled with the excitement of her first adventure collecting mussels beneath the thick sea ice.

Bailey, Donna. *Nomads and Cities.* Austin, TX: Steck-Vaughn, 1990.
A clever book that presents traditional nomads, such as the Bedouin, and extends the concept to moderns, such as circus performers, ship crews, etc.

Bang, Molly. *The Grey Lady and the Strawberry Snatcher.* New York: Four Winds Press, 1984.
A magical wordless fantasy that follows the Grey Lady's clever and surprising methods of eluding the Strawberry Snatcher, who is always close.

Bang, Molly. *The Paper Crane.* New York: Greenwillow, 1985.
A hungry stranger brings new life to a fading restaurant in this story of generosity rewarded; based on an ancient folktale.

Baylor, Byrd. *Before You Came This Way* (illustrated by Tom Bahti). New York: E.P. Dutton, 1969. Out of print.
Prehistoric Indian rock drawings tell us of people who once lived on Earth.

Baylor, Byrd. *Everybody Needs a Rock.* New York: Atheneum, 1985.

Baylor, Byrd. *The Way to Start a Day* (illustrated by Peter Parnall). New York: Aladdin, 1977.

Bourke, Linda. *Handmade ABC.* New York: Harper & Row, 1981. Out of print.
Clear illustrations show how to hand sign each letter of the alphabet.

Children's Television Workshop (with Linda Bove). *Sign Language Fun* (illustrated by Tom Cooke). New York: Random House, 1980.
Photographs illustrate how to sign many words familiar and important to young children.

Clifton, Lucille. *The Boy Who Didn't Believe in Spring* (illustrated by Brinton Turkle). New York: E.P. Dutton, 1973.
Finding signs of spring in the city can be a difficult task, but doubters King Shabazz and Tony Polito set out to try.

Cooney, Barbara. *Miss Rumphius.* New York: Viking Penguin, 1985.
An independent young girl listens to her grandfather's advice and her own dreams. She travels the world, in old age lives by the sea, and eventually finds her own special way to make the world more beautiful.

Cooney, Nancy Evans. *The Wobbly Tooth* (illustrated by Marylin Hafner). New York: G.P. Putnam's Sons, 1978. Out of print.

A loose tooth continues to annoy Elizabeth Ann throughout her spirited day.

Cummings, Pat. *Jimmy Lee Did It.* New York: Lothrop, Lee & Shepard, 1985. Out of print.

Brother Artie blames Jimmy Lee for all kinds of disasters and evil deeds; but when Angel tries to catch him, he's always a step ahead of her.

de Paola, Tomie. *Watch Out for the Chicken Feet in Your Soup.* Englewood Cliffs, NJ: Prentice-Hall, 1985.

Joey is jealous when his grandma gives his friend too much attention.

Dragonwagon, Crescent. *Half a Moon and One Whole Star* (illustrated by Jerry Pinkney). New York: Macmillan, 1986.

A wonderful soothing rhythm pulses through the night as Susan falls asleep and the creatures and people of the night awake.

Father Gander (Dr. Douglas W. Larche). *Father Gander Nursery Rhymes* (illustrated by Carolyn). Advocacy Press, P.O. Box 236, Santa Barbara, CA 93102, 1985.

People seem to react strongly one way or the other to this rewrite of Mother Goose rhymes. Verses added to the original rhymes give equal time to both sexes. Illustrations superbly reflect diversity and include handicapped children—for this alone, it deserves kudos.

Gauch, Patricia Lee. *Christina Katerina & The Box* (illustrated by Doris Burn). New York: Coward, McCann & Geoghegan, 1971.

Christina has plenty of imagination as she and her friend Fats explore the play potential of a large cardboard carton.

Graham, Bob. *The Red Woolen Blanket.* Boston: Little, Brown, 1987.

A story of a girl's attachment to her security blanket; a universal issue described with a unique Australian flavor.

Graw, J.S. *La ratita presumida [The Little Conceited Rat].* Barcelona, Spain: Ediciones Hymsa, 1989. Other titles in the series: *Las 7 ovejas y el lobe [The Seven Sheep and the Wolf],* *Los tres osos [The Three Bears].*

Charming pastel colors and a simple and fluid text make these popular stories a special treat for the little ones.

Greene, Jacqueline Dembar. *Nathan's Hanukkah Bargain* (illustrated by Steffi Karen Rubin). Kar-Ben Copies, Inc., 6800 Tildenwood Lane, Rockville, MD 20852, 1986.

Nathan invites his grandfather to help him shop for a menorah, but it takes some effort and a little bargaining to find just the right one.

Greenfield, Eloise. *Darlene* (illustrated by George Ford). New York: Methuen, 1980.

Greenfield, Eloise. *Daydreamers* (illustrated by Tom Feelings). New York: Dial Books for Young Readers, 1985.

Intriguing sketches of Black children fill out the poem's images of children who pause for reflection.

Greenfield, Eloise. *First Pink Light* (illustrated by Moneta Barnett). New York: Scholastic, 1976. Out of print.

Greenfield, Eloise. *Me & Neesie* (illustrated by Moneta Barnett). New York: Thomas Y. Crowell, 1975.

Haller, Danita Ross. *Not Just Any Ring* (illustrated by Deborah Kogan Ray). New York: Alfred A. Knopf, 1982. Out of print.

With the help of her wise grandfather, Jesse learns that she must make her own magic and her own good days.

Hazen, Barbara Shook. *Tight Times* (illustrated by Trina Schart Hyman). New York: Penguin Books, 1979.

A young boy faces the daily realities of his family's economic struggles.

Head, Barry, and Jim Seguin. *Who Am I?* (photographs by Frank Dastolfo). Family Communications, Inc., 4802 Fifth Avenue, Pittsburgh, PA, 15213, 1975.

Beautiful color photographs celebrate all the me's of a young girl—daughter, gardener, adventurer, student, friend. She also wears a hearing aid.

Highwater, Jamake. *Moonsong Lullaby* (illustrated by Marcia Keegan). New York: Lothrop, Lee & Shepard, 1981. Out of print.

This lullaby fills us with images of the natural wonders of the night as American Indians once knew it.

Hill, Elizabeth Starr. *Evan's Corner* (illustrated by Nancy Grossman). New York: Holt, Rinehart and Winston, 1967. Out of print.

In such a large family, Evan longs for a place of his own to fix up just as he wants it and to enjoy some peace and quiet.

Hill, Eric. *La hermanita de Spot [Spot's Little Sister]*. New York: G.P. Putnam's Sons, 1989.

Spot learns to live with his new sister, Susie, and decides that she is fun to have around.

Hines, Anna Grossnickle. *Daddy Makes the Best Spaghetti.* New York: Clarion, 1986.

Daddy has a way of turning everyday routines into delightful games.

Hughes, Shirley. *George the Babysitter.* Englewood Cliffs, NJ: Prentice-Hall, 1975. Out of print.

The children help babysitter George make it through a busy day's activities.

Isadora, Rachel. *Ben's Trumpet.* New York: Greenwillow, 1979.

Set in the 1920s, this is the story of a young musician who feels the music and yearns to be part of it.

Isadora, Rachel. *City Seen from A to Z.* New York: Greenwillow, 1983.

Images of city life and the variety of its people fill this alphabet book.

Isadora, Rachel. *Max.* New York: Collier, 1976.

Max, star baseball player, discovers that ballet class is a great pregame warm-up on Saturday mornings.

Jeffers, Susan. *Brother Eagle, Sister Sky.* New York: Dial Books, 1991.

Jeffers has taken Chief Seattle's famous speech and reworked it to create an elegant, appealing picture book for children.

Jensen, Virginia Allen. *Sara and the Door* (illustrated by Ann Strugnell). New York: Harper & Row, 1977. Out of print.

Sara experiences the satisfaction that comes with solving a problem by herself.

Jonas, Ann. *The Quilt.* New York: Greenwillow, 1984.

A quilt made of scraps from her family's wardrobe keeps Sally awake.

Jonas, Ann. *The Trek.* New York: Greenwillow, 1985.

Two girls brave wild jungle adventures together on the way to school.

Keats, Ezra Jack. *Dreams.* New York: Collier, 1992.

Late one night, Roberto sends his paper mouse on quite an adventure.

Keats, Ezra Jack. *Goggles!* New York: Collier, 1969.

Keats, Ezra Jack. *Jennie's Hat.* New York: Harper & Row, 1985.

Keats, Ezra Jack. *Louie.* New York: Scholastic, 1975. Out of print.

Keats, Ezra Jack. *Pet Show!* New York: Collier, 1972.

Keats, Ezra Jack. *Peter's Chair.* New York: Harper & Row, 1983.

Keats, Ezra Jack. *Regards to the Man in the Moon.* New York: Four Winds Press, 1984.

Keats, Ezra Jack. *Whistle for Willie.* New York: The Viking Press, 1964.

Keyworth, C.L. *New Day.* New York: Morrow, 1986.

Moving is a disturbing experience for young Mandy, but she soon finds happiness in her new racially integrated town and school.

Klagsbrun, Francine (ed.). *Free to Be . . . You and Me.* New York: McGraw-Hill, 1974. Out of print.

The stories and songs in both the record and book are delightful in their strong male and female characters. A storytelling, read-aloud resource.

Lalli, Judy. *Feelings Alphabet.* B.L. Winch & Associates, 45 Hitching Post Drive, Building 2, Rolling Hills Estates, CA 90274, 1984.

An alphabet of emotions, which all people share, captured in photographs.

Little, Lessie Jones, and Eloise Greenfield. *I Can Do It By Myself* (illustrated by Carole Byard). New York: Thomas Y. Crowell, 1978.

Setting out by himself to buy a birthday gift for his mother gives Donald a special feeling of pride.

Locker, Thomas. *The Land of the Gray Wolf.* New York: Dial Books, 1991.

A Native American perspective on the man-nature relationship as it has developed since the arrival of European-Americans.

Mendoza, George. *Need A House? Call Ms. Mouse!* (illustrated by Doris Susan Smith). New York: Grosset & Dunlap, 1981. Out of print.

Henrietta Mouse, world-famous decorator, designs very special homes for her animal friends.

Meyer, Linda D. *Harriet Tubman: They Called Me Moses.* Seattle: Parenting Press, 1988.

Written in slightly dialectical English, Harriet tells of her life as a slave and as a conductor on the Underground Railroad.

Munsch, Robert N. *The Paper Bag Princess* (illustrated by Michael Martchenko). Toronto, Canada: Annick Press Ltd. (distributed by Firefly Books Ltd., 3520 Pharmacy Avenue, Unit 1–C, Scarborough, Ontario M1W 2T8), 1980.

In fairy-tale style Munsch creates a princess who sets out to rescue a prince and then is not all that pleased with her prize.

Pogrebin, Letty Cottin (ed.). *Stories for Free Children.* New York: McGraw-Hill, 1982. Out of print.

A collection of stories that reflect diversity and cross barriers. A read-aloud or storytelling resource.

Pomerantz, Charlotte. *The Tamarindo Puppy and Other Poems* (illustrated by Byron Barton). New York: Greenwillow, 1980.

Poems with English and Spanish words and lines mixed together.

Quinsey, Mary Beth. *Why Does That Man Have Such a Big Nose?* (photographs by Wilson Chan). Parenting Press, Inc., 7744 31st Avenue. N.E., Seattle, WA 98115, 1986.

Questions children often ask about physical differences are answered straightforwardly. Also a good reference for teachers.

Romanova, Natalia. *Once There Was a Tree.* New York: Dial Books, 1985.

Originally published in the Soviet Union, this book has the potential to build bridges of international understanding. It concludes that, "The tree belongs to all, because it grows from the earth that is home for all."

Schlank, Carol H. and Barbara Metzker. *Martin Luther King, Jr.: A Biography for Young Children.* Henrietta, NY: Rochester Association for the Education of Young Children, Box 356, Henrietta, NY 14467, 1989.

This celebration of Martin Luther King, Jr., traces his life, from his childhood to his growth into a strong, heroic man.

Schubert, Ingrid and Dieter. *El monstruo de las fresas [The Monster of the Strawberries].* Barcelona, Spain: Editorial Lumen, 1989.

A little girl helps the monsters of the strawberry garden get rid of a thief who is stealing all the strawberries.

Schweitzer, Byrd Baylor. *Amigo* (illustrated by Garth Williams). New York: Collier, 1963.

Francisco, a boy, and Amigo, a prairie dog, both long to have a pet—so they team up!

Schweitzer, Byrd Baylor. *One Small Blue Bead.* New York: Macmillan, 1965. Out of print.

The discovery of a blue bead takes us back to ancient times and a small boy who aids an old man's search for other men.

Scott, Ann Herbert. *On Mother's Lap* (illustrated by Glo Coalson). New York: McGraw-Hill, 1972. Out of print.

Michael learns that there's always room on mother's lap, even for a baby sister. Illustrations depict Eskimo life.

Scott, Ann Herbert. *Sam* (illustrated by Symeon Shimin). New York: McGraw-Hill, 1967. Out of print.

When Sam just can't take being left out any more, his family responds with a job that's just perfect for him.

Spier, Peter. *People.* New York: Doubleday, 1980.

A beautiful book that discusses and celebrates the scope of human diversity—appearance, wealth, ability, preferences, religion—and the commonalties that bind us together.

Steptoe, John. *Daddy Is a Monster . . . Sometimes.* New York: Harper & Row Junior Books Group, 1983.

His children can turn this daddy into a monster when they push him too far.

Suárez, Maribel. *Los colores [Colors].* Mexico City: Editorial Grijalbo, 1989.

This book introduces children to colors, the concept of opposites, basic geometric shapes, and numbers 1–10.

Waber, Bernard. *Ira Sleeps Over.* Boston, MA: Houghton Mifflin, 1972.

Ira has a difficult time deciding whether or not to take his teddy bear along on his overnight at Reggie's house.

Wagener, Gerda. *Billy y Tigre [Billy and Tiger].* Madrid, Spain: Ediciones SM, 1989.

Billy, a kitten, and Tigre, a baby tiger, are close friends, and when the disparity in their sizes becomes larger and larger, they become part of a circus show.

Waterton, Betty. *A Salmon for Simon* (illustrated by Ann Blades). Vancouver, BC: Douglas & McIntyre (distributed by Firefly Books, 250 Sparks Avenue, Willowdale, Ontario, Canada M2H 2S4), 1992.

Simon spends his summer fishing for a salmon. Then, just when he gives up, he catches one in a most unusual way.

Welber, Robert. *The Train* (illustrated by Deborah Ray). New York: Pantheon, 1972. Out of print.

One of the few books depicting a biracial family. Story of a young girl whose love of trains eventually overcomes her fears of the journey to watch them.

Wilhelm, Hans. *Yo siempre to querré [I Will Always Love You].* Barcelona, Spain: Editorial Juventud, 1989.

A little boy tells a story about the adventures he has shared with his dog Elfi as they have grown up together.

Williams, Barbara. *Kevin's Grandma* (illustrated by Kay Chorao). New York: Scholastic, 1975. Out of print.

Kevin tells stories of adventures with his grandma that would make anyone envious—but could he be exaggerating?

Williams, Vera B. *A Chair for My Mother.* New York: Greenwillow, 1982.

Fire destroyed their possessions, so a girl and her mother and grandmother work together to save for an overstuffed chair in which to relax and snuggle.

Williams, Vera B. *Cherries and Cherry Pits.* New York: Greenwillow, 1986.

Through her drawings and stories, Bidemmi creates a very special and unusual way of drawing humankind together.

Williams, Vera B. *Something Special for Me.* New York: Mulberry, 1983.

Yarbrough, Camille. *Cornrows* (illustrated by Carole Byard). New York: Coward-McCann, 1979. Out of print.

As Mama and Great-Grammaw braid their children's hair, stories are woven, too, about meanings behind the patterns in celebration of the Black tradition.

Yashima, Taro. *Umbrella.* New York: The Viking Press, 1958.

When Momo gets a new umbrella, it's very hard to wait for rain—and then, such joy!

Special relationships

Barrett, Judi. *Cloudy With a Chance of Meatballs* (illustrated by Ron Barrett). New York: Atheneum, 1982.

Grandpa has a lively imagination that almost brings his tall tale to life.

Caines, Jeannette. *Daddy* (illustrated by Ronald Himler). New York: Harper & Row, 1977. Out of print.

Weekend visits with her father are full of comfortable playfulness and dependable delight for Windy.

Caines, Jeannette. *Just Us Women* (illustrated by Pat Cummings). New York: Harper & Row, 1984.

Caines, Jeannette. *Window Wishing* (illustrated by Kevin Brooks). New York: Harper & Row, 1980.

Flournoy, Valerie. *The Patchwork Quilt* (illustrated by Jerry Pinkney). New York: Dial Books for Young Readers, 1985.

Creating a quilt helps Tanya and her grandmother weave the past and present together to tell the story of their family.

Fox, Mem. *Wilfrid Gordon McDonald Partridge* (illustrated by Julie Vivas). New York: Kane/Miller, 1985.

This is my favorite book about friendship across generations—a charming story of how a young boy helps his older friend find her memories.

Hest, Amy. *The Crack-of-Dawn Walkers* (illustrated by Amy Schwartz). New York: Macmillan, 1984.

A Sunday morning walk with her grandfather is a very special time for Sadie.

Johnson, Angela. *Do Like Kyla*. New York: Orchard Books, 1990.

A positive sibling relationship between two non-White sisters.

Keats, Ezra Jack. *Apt. 3*. New York: Macmillan, 1971.

Curiosity about a neighbor and his music lead Sam and Ben to a new friend.

Mahy, Margaret. *Ultra-Violet Catastrophe!* (illustrated by Brian Froud). New York: Parents' Magazine Press, 1975.

Sally and Great-Uncle Magnus are two of a kind, and their friendship develops during a walk together.

Martin, Bill, Jr. and John Archambault. *Knots on a Counting Rope*. New York: Henry Holt, 1987.

This tale of a blind boy and his grandfather captures the warmth, intimacy, and integrity of the Native American tradition.

Miles, Miska. *Annie and the Old One* (illustrated by Peter Parnall). Boston, MA: Little, Brown, 1971.

Annie's love for the Old One makes it difficult for her to let go, but eventually she comes to understand that aging and dying are a natural part of living.

Omerod, Jan. *Reading; Sleeping; Dad's Back;* and *Messy Baby*. New York: Lothrop, Lee, & Shepard, 1985.

This series of books portrays the very close and natural relationship between a baby and his father.

Ricklen, Neil. *Grandma and Me; Grandpa and Me; Daddy and Me; Mommy and Me*. New York: Simon & Schuster/Little Simon Super Chubby board books, 1988.

Lovely interactions between grandparents and children, and parents and children.

Steptoe, John. *Stevie*. New York: Harper & Row, 1986.

Sometimes a younger child—even a playmate—can seem like a nuisance until he moves away.

Stevenson, James. *We Hate Rain!* New York: Greenwillow, 1988.

During a dreary rainy spell, Grandpa tells grandchildren Mary Anne and Louie what *real* rain was like in his day.

Viorst, Judith. *Rosie and Michael* (illustrated by Lorna Tomei). New York: Atheneum, 1988.

Best friends Rosie and Michael enjoy and understand each other, for better or for worse.

Wittman, Sally. *A Special Trade* (illustrated by Karen Gundersheimer). New York: Harper & Row, 1985.

Nelly and Bartholomew are neighbors of very different ages, special friends who take turns caring for each other.

Books for infants and toddlers reflecting diversity

Ahlberg, Janet and Allan. *The Baby's Catalogue.* Boston, MA: Little, Brown, 1982.

Bang, Molly. *Ten, Nine, Eight.* New York: Greenwillow, 1983.

Crews, Donald. *Bicycle Race.* New York: Greenwillow, 1985.

Dijs, Cala. *Are You My Mommy? A Pop-Up Book.* New York: Simon and Schuster, 1990.
    Provides an opportunity to reveal to children the varying types of family structures.

Gilbert, Yvonne. *Baby's Book of Lullabies and Cradle Songs.* New York: Dial Books, 1990.
    Includes 16 traditional songs from the United States, England, and Europe, along with lovely illustrations.

Hughes, Shirley. *When We Went to the Park.* New York: Lothrop, Lee & Shepard, 1985.

Jonas, Ann. *When You Were a Baby.* New York: Greenwillow, 1982.

Keats, Ezra Jack. *The Snowy Day.* New York: The Viking Press, 1962.

Miller, Margaret. *Whose Shoe.* New York: Greenwillow, 1991.
    Miller has included both children and adult "shoe wearers" and a range of people from all walks of life, including a multiracial couple, which makes the book especially appealing for a wide audience.

O'Brien, Anne Sibley. *Come Play with Us.* New York: Holt, Rinehart and Winston, 1985.

O'Brien, Anne Sibley. *I'm Not Tired.* New York: Holt, Rinehart and Winston, 1985.

Ormerod, Jan. *Dad's Back.* New York: Lothrop, Lee & Shepard, 1985. Also *Messy Baby, Reading, Sleeping,* and *Young Joe.*

Williams, Vera B. *"More, more, more," Said the Baby: 3 Love Stories.* New York: Greenwillow, 1990.
    This book has it all: racial diversity, nice language, and lovely artwork.

Life in other places

• Africa
Feelings, Muriel. *Jambo Means Hello: Swahili Alphabet Book* (illustrated by Tom Feelings). New York: Dial Books for Young Readers, 1974.

Feelings, Muriel. *Moja Means One* (illustrated by Tom Feelings). New York: The Dial Press, 1971.

Graham, Lorenz. *Song of the Boat* (illustrated by Leo and Diane Dillon). New York: Thomas Y. Crowell, 1975.

• The Caribbean
Lessac, Frane. *My Little Island.* New York: J.B. Lippincott, 1985. Out of print.

• India
Bonnici, Peter. *The Festival* (illustrated by Lisa Kopper). Carolrhoda Books, 241 First Avenue North, Minneapolis, MN 55401, 1985. Also *The First Rains.*

• South Africa
Lewin, Hugh. *Jafta* (illustrated by Lisa Kopper). Minneapolis, MN: Carolrhoda Books, 1983. Also *Jafta and the Wedding, Jafta—The Journey, Jafta—The Town, Jafta's Father,* and *Jafta's Mother*

• Around the World
Abells, Chana Byers. *The Children We Remember.* New York: Greenwillow, 1983.
    A moving account of the Holocaust told through photographs of its children.

Anno, Mitsumasa, et al. *All in a Day.* New York: Philomel, 1986.
    Nine celebrated artists have brought the world's children together in this work of friendship and peace. Activities, time, and season in eight different countries are illustrated over a 24-hour period, accentuating ways in which we are all alike.

Bailey, Donna. *Where We Live Series: Australia; Hong Kong; India;* and *Trinidad.* Madison, NJ: Steck-Vaughn, 1990.

A glimpse of occupations, lifestyles, climate, recreation, and animals of particular countries via the perspective of a young child narrator.

Bauer, Caroline F. (Ed.). *Snowy Day Stories and Poems.* New York: Lippincott, 1986.

A retelling of snowy day stories from faraway places, including a Russian folktale and a lovely Japanese story.

Feeney, Stephanie. *A is for Aloha* (photographs by Hella Hammid). Honolulu: The University Press of Hawaii, 1980.

A beautiful alphabet book with black-and-white photographs of Hawaiian life.

Feeney, Stephanie. *Hawaii Is a Rainbow.* Honolulu: University of Hawaii Press, 1985.

The vibrant colors of the Hawaiian Islands are perfectly captured in this gorgeous book about the diversity of our 50th state.

Goldfarb, Mace, M.D. *Fighters, Refugees, Immigrants: A Story of the Hmong.* Minneapolis, MN: Carolrhoda Books, 1982.

Although the text is written for older children, the color photographs of life in a refugee camp in Thailand are an important resource.

Koss, Amy G. *City Critters Around the World.* Los Angeles: Price Stern Sloan, 1991.

Young children will delight in the hedgehogs in Edinburgh, the storks in Katmandu, and the camels in Karachi as they journey to these settings.

Raynor, Dorka. *Grandparents Around the World.* Chicago: Albert Whitman, 1977. Out of print.

Raynor, Dorka. *My Friends Live in Many Places.* Chicago: Albert Whitman, 1980. Out of print.

Rogers, Jean. *Runaway Mittens.* New York: Greenwillow, 1988.

An Alaskan boy, Pica, pursues his runaway mittens in his native Alaskan environment complete with ice fishing, sled dogs, and a one-room schoolhouse.

Rylant, Cynthia. *When I Was Young in the Mountains* (illustrated by Diane Goode). New York: E.P. Dutton, 1982.

Beautiful images of a childhood in Appalachia.

Smith, MaryLou M. *Grandmother's Adobe Dollhouse* (illustrated by Ann Blackstone). New Mexico Magazine, The Joseph Montoya Building, 1100 St. Francis Drive, Santa Fe, NM 87503, 1984.

Not exactly another place, but this book shares information about Pueblo Indians and the culture of New Mexico.

Steiner, Barbara. *Whale Brother.* New York: Walker, 1988.

Omu, an Eskimo boy and aspiring carver, will inspire in children a respect for the Eskimo lifestyle.

Svend, Otto S. (translated by Joan Tate). *Children of the Yangtze River.* London: Pelham Books Ltd. (distributed by Merrimack Publishers' Circle, 47 Pelham Road, Salem, NH 03079), 1985.

Trinca, Rod, and Kerry Argent. *One Wooly Wombat* (illustrated by Kerry Argent). New York: Kane/Miller, 1982.

A delightful counting book with Australian flavor.

Vaughn, Jenny. *Greece and Russia.* Madison, NJ: Steck-Vaughn, 1990.

A glimpse of occupations, lifestyles, climate, recreation, and animals of particular countries via the perspective of a young child narrator.

Vernon, Adele (retold by). *The Riddle.* New York: Dodd, Mead, 1987.

An insight into life and culture of medieval Europe.

Walter, Mildred Pitts. *Habari Gani?* New York: Lothrop, Lee & Shepard, 1989.

This novel, intended for staff to read to children, teaches about the African-American holiday, Kwanzaa.

Williams, Vera B. *Stringbean's Trip to the Shining Sea.* New York: Greenwillow, 1988.

Geography of sorts that's much more fun than what's found in children's textbooks.

Books about diversity

• Biracial

Adoff, Arnold. *Black is Brown is Tan* (illustrated by Emily McCully). New York: Harper & Row, 1992.

A story-poem about a house full of love and adults and children of many colors.

Mandelbaum, Pili. *You Be Me, I'll Be You.* Brooklyn, NY: Kane/Miller, P.O. Box 529, Brooklyn, NY 11231, 1990.

A White father and a Black daughter try to work through the problem of not liking your looks.

Rosenberg, Maxine B. *Living in Two Worlds* (photographs by George Ancona). New York: Lothrop, Lee & Shepard, 1986.

Biracial children share their feelings about themselves and their heritage and the prejudices they encounter. Wonderful photographs—a great variety of ethnic and racial mixtures.

• Disabilities

Baker, Pamela J. *My First Book of Sign.* Washington, DC: Gallaudet University Press, 1986.

This book for hearing children about deaf people's language will open the door to new forms of communication.

Brown, Tricia. *Someone Special, Just Like You* (photographs by Fran Ortiz). New York: Henry Holt, 1991.

Cairo, Shelley. *Our Brother Has Down's Syndrome* (photographs by Irene McNeil). Toronto, Canada: Annick Press (distributed by Firefly Books, 3520 Pharmacy Avenue, Unit 1-C, Scarborough, Ontario, Canada M1W 2T8), 1985.

Chapman, Elizabeth. *Suzy* (illustrated by Margery Gill). The Bodley Head Ltd., 9 Bow Street, London, England WC2E7AL, 1982.

Corrigan, Kathy. *Emily Umily* (illustrated by Vlasta van Kampen). Toronto, Canada: Annick Press Ltd., 1984.

Peterson, Jeanne Whitehouse. *I Have a Sister—My Sister is Deaf* (illustrated by Deborah Ray). New York: Harper & Row, 1984.

• Family composition

Bauer, Caroline Feller. *My Mom Travels A Lot* (illustrated by Nancy Winslow Parker). New York: Frederick Warne, 1981.

Christiansen, C.B. *My Mother's House, My Father's House.* New York: Atheneum, 1989.

Warm, bright illustrations and a positive tone make this book useful for exploring children's feelings about their lives with separated parents.

Levinson, Riki. *I Go With My Family to Grandma's.* New York: Dutton, 1986.

It's around 1900, and a young, burgeoning New York family converge via bicycle, train, trolley, wagon, and car to their grandmother's house. Learn about old New York!

Livingston, Myra C. *There Was a Place and Other Poems.* New York: Macmillan, 1988.

Children who are groping and coping with new "broken" family situations may relate to these brief poems.

Perry, Patricia, and Marietta Lynch. *Mommy and Daddy Are Divorced.* New York: Dial Books for Young Readers, 1985.

Rice, Melanie and Chris. *All About Me.* Garden City, NY: Doubleday, 1987.

Many types of families are acknowledged with varying parental situations, homes, food, and other qualities not normally depicted in children's literature.

Rosenberg, Maxine B. *Being a Twin, Having a Twin* (photographs by George Ancona). New York: Lothrop, Lee & Shepard, 1985.

Simon, Norma. *All Kinds of Families* (illustrated by Joe Lasker). Chicago: Albert Whitman, 1976.

•Multicultural

Hoyt-Goldsmith. *Totem Pole.* New York: Holiday House, 1990.

About a young Northwest Coast Indian boy who works with his father to carve and paint a totem pole for a tribal reservation.

Levinson, Riki. *Our Home Is the Sea.* New York: Dutton, 1988.

A young boy is sent to school to fulfill his mother's hope that he become a schoolteacher instead of following his dream to become a fisherman in Hong Kong harbor like his father and grandfather.

Macmillan, Dianne, and Dorothy Freeman. *My Best Friend Duc Tran: Meeting a Vietnamese-American Family.* New York: Julian Messner, 1987.

An informative look at a Vietnamese American family.

Polacco, Patricia. *The Keeping Quilt.* New York: Simon & Schuster, 1988.

A glimpse into the lives of Russian immigrants to America—not as an idealized fairytale, but realistically, with all of the anomalies, imperfections, and richness of their culture.

Shalant, Phyllis. *Look What We've Brought You From Vietnam: Crafts, Games, Recipes, Stories, and Other Cultural Activities From New Americans.* New York: Julian Messner, 1988.

An activity book for 6-, 7-, and 8-year olds that teaches Vietnamese culture in a fun, creative manner.

• Sex roles and stereotypes

English, Betty. *Women at Their Work.* New York: Dial, 1988.

Meet a variety of working women, including a dentist, a launch operator, a judge, a chef, a painter, a firefighter, and many more.

Kempler, Susan, Doreen Rappaport, and Michele Spirn. *A Man Can Be . . .* (photographs by Russel Dian). Human Sciences Press, 233 Spring Street, New York, NY 10013, 1981.

Merriam, Eve. *Boys & Girls, Girls & Boys* (illustrated by Harriet Sherman). New York: Holt, Rinehart and Winston, 1972. Out of print.

Merriam, Eve. *Mommies at Work.* New York: Simon & Schuster, 1989.

This book gives children in child care programs some insight into why they are there, and what their mothers do when they're away.

Nicki, Peter. *The Story of a Kind of Wolf.* New York: North-South Books, 1988.

Combat stereotypes with this book about a gentle wolf and a silly owl.

Portnoy, Mindy Avra. *Ima on the Bima* (illustrated by Steffi Karen Rubin). Kar-Ben Copies, Inc., 6800 Tildenwood Lane, Rockville, MD 20852, 1986.

Winthrop, Elizabeth. *Tough Eddie.* New York: Dutton, 1985.

Eddie appears to be a tough guy, but his sensitive side is revealed when his friends discover he has a dollhouse.

• Tales and legends

In addition to the following, don't forget the wealth of other beautiful and interesting legends from around the world.

Baden, Robert. *Y Domingo, siete [And Sunday Makes Seven].* Niles, IL: Albert Whitman, 1990.

This Costa Rican folktale about the 12 witches who reward Carlos for his help with their song about the days of the week is presented in a well-done translation.

Birdseye, Tom. *A Song of Stars.* New York: Holiday House, 1990.

A retelling of a Chinese myth that is the basis of traditional festivals in both China and Japan.

Hamilton, Virginia (told by). *In the Beginning: Creation Stories From Around the World.* New York: Harcourt Brace Jovanovich, 1988.

Learning how different cultures view the earth's beginnings will give children insight into different philosophies and foster a universal sense of wonder about the mysteries of the universe.

Kimmel, Eric A. (retold by). *Baba Yaga. A Russian Folktale.* New York: Holiday House, 1991.

The heroine in this story succeeds through obedience and civility, in contrast to others who exhibit selfishness, injustice, trickery, and unkindness.

San Souci, Robert D. (retold by). *The Enchanted Tapestry*. New York: Dial Books for Young Readers, 1987.

A Chinese folktale about a young boy's fidelity to his aging mother.

Sierra, Judy and Robert Kaminski. *Multicultural Folktales: Stories To Tell Young Children*. Phoenix, AZ: The Oryx Press, 1991.

Emphasizing a multicultural approach, each of these 25 stories and rhymes identifies the country or area of origin.

Stewig, John W. (retold by). *Stone Soup*. New York: Holiday House, 1991.

This new version has a girl as the heroine who uses the familiar ploy to feed herself.

Torre, Betty L. (retold by). *The Luminous Pearl*. New York: Orchard Books, 1990.

A Chinese folktale about a young hero who keeps his promise to rescue desperate people even though he risks missing his chance to win the beautiful princess.

Recordings

Avni, Fran. *A Child's Look at . . . What It Means To Be Jewish*. Cassette. Kid's Records. Distributed by Alcazar, Inc., Box 429, Waterbury, VT 05676, 1986.

Geared toward second graders and up, this recording presents a panorama of Jewish history through conversations among family members, both young and old.

Avni, Fran. *Mostly Matzah*. Cassette. Lemonstone Records. Distributed by Alcazar, Inc., Box 429, Waterbury, VT 05676, 1986.

The story of Hebrew people escaping from slavery in Egypt; recommended for use during the Jewish festival of Passover.

Hayes, Joe. *Coyote and Native American Folk Tales*. Cassette. Santa Fe, NM: Trails West Publishing, 1983.

Tales of Coyote, the traditional Native American hero who manages to come out on top in one hair-raising adventure after another.

Locke, Kevin. *Lakota/Dakota Flute Music*. Cassette. Featherstone, P.O. Box 487, Brookings, SD 57006, 1983.

A collection of flute melodies that were used in courting rituals among traditional society of the Lakota/Dakota Indians.

Music for Little People. *Shake Sugaree*. Cassette. P.O. Box 1460, Redway, CA 95560, 1988.

Taj Majal sings traditional family tunes from many parts of the world.

Round River Records. *I'm Gonna Let It Shine—A Gathering of Voices for Freedom*. Cassette and compact disk. 301 Jacob Street, Seekork, MA 02771.

A musical introduction for young children to the extraordinary emotional impact of the civil rights movement and our ongoing struggles for freedom.

Tickle Tune Typhoon. *All of Us Will Shine*. Cassette. P.O. Box 15153, Seattle, WA 98115.

The theme song, *All of Us Will Shine*, is a celebration of individual differences.

Tickle Tune Typhoon. *Hug the Earth*. Album. P.O. Box 15153, Seattle, WA 98115, 1985.

Included in this album are traditional selections such as "If You're Happy," and superb multicultural pieces such as "On Cedar Tree," an authentic Native American chant.

Tickle Tune Typhoon. *Let's Be Friends*. Video cassette. P.O. Box 15153, Seattle, WA 98115, 1989.

Themes of friendship, racial equality, self-health and -care, appreciation for different abilities, and environmental awareness form the core of this release.

Within Your Reach—
Resources on Diversity for
Adults*

Abbott, Carole F., and Susan Gold. Conferring With Parents When You're Concerned That Their Child Needs Special Services. *Young Children, 46*(4), 10–14. 1991.

Anastasiow, N.J. *Development and Disability: A Psychobiological Analysis for Special Educators.* Baltimore, Md.: Brookes, 1986.

According to the author's psychobiological perspective, outcome for all children is dependent on the critical interplay between their genetic makeup and their environment. Anastasiow shows how this fundamental concept applies to many areas of development and explains how it serves as the basis of early intervention for children with special needs.

Austin, M.C., and E.C. Jenkins. *Promoting World Understanding Through Literature, K–8.* Littleton, CO: Libraries Unlimited, 1983.

This excellent aid provides assistance in selecting books about the following ethnic groups both in and outside the United States: African Americans, Native North Americans, and Mexicans and Mexican-Americans.

Beginning Equal Project. *Beginning Equal: A Manual About Nonsexist Childrearing for Infants and Toddlers.* New York: Women's Action Alliance and Pre-School Association, 1983.

A series of workshop materials designed to help caregivers and/or parents explore gender issues as they affect very young children. These workshops grew out of the research project with the same name; topics include exploring your own sex-role attitudes, adult-child interactions, identifying conflicts and developing strategies for change, and analyzing toys and materials. Alternative workshop formats included. Workshop materials also available in Spanish.

Bernstein, Bonnie, and Leigh Blair. *North American Crafts Workshop.* Belmont, CA: David S. Lake Publishers, 1982. Out of print.

Craft ideas to use with young children.

Billman, Jane. The Native American Curriculum: Attempting Alternatives to Tepees and Headbands. *Young Children, 47*(6), 22–25. 1992.

Boston Women's Health Book Collective. *Ourselves and Our Children.* New York: Random House, 1978. Out of print.

Exploring families and parenting—the diversity, issues, and richness.

---

*Books described as "out of print" may still be available from a library. Letters to the publisher requesting reprinting are helpful in letting publishers know that some of us want—and will buy—these little-known but valuable books.

Brady, Phyllis. Columbus and the Quincentennial Myths: Another Side of the Story. *Young Children, 47*(6), 4–14. 1992.

Bricker, D.D. *Early Education of At-Risk and Handicapped Infants, Toddlers, and Preschool Children.* Glenview, Ill.: Scott, Foresman, 1986.
This book is distinct from others dealing with early childhood special education because it focuses on practical early intervention strategies rather than merely discussing concepts of early development across domains in children with special needs.

Caston, Don. *Easy-to-Make Aids for Your Handicapped Child: A Guide for Parents and Teachers.* Englewood Cliffs, NJ: Prentice-Hall, 1981. Out of print.
How-to plans for building and customizing aids for children with special needs such as back rests, toilets, climbing frames, and walkers.

Caughey, Carol. Becoming the Child's Ally—Observations in a Classroom for Children Who Have Been Abused. *Young Children, 46*(4), 22–28. 1991.

Chenfeld, Mimi B. From Catatonic to Hyperactive: Randy Snapped Today. *Young Children, 44*(4), 25–27. 1989.

Children's Foundation. *Helping Children Love Themselves and Others: A Professional Handbook for Family Day Care.* 725 15th Street, N.W., Suite 505, Washington, DC 20005. 1990.
Stresses the antibias, multicultural approach. Includes activities for children and a resource guide.

Children's Foundation. *Helping Children Love Themselves and Others: A Resource Guide to Equity Materials for Young Children.* 725 15th Street, N.W., Suite 505, Washington, DC 20005. 1990.
Contains an annotated bibliography of children's books and adult resources. Lists companies that supply antibias, multicultural materials.

Clark, Leilani, Sheridan DeWolf, and Carl Clark. Teaching Teachers to Avoid Having Culturally Assaultive Classrooms. *Young Children, 47*(5), 4–9. 1992.

Clay, James W. Working With Lesbian and Gay Parents and Their Children. *Young Children, 45*(3), 31–35. 1990.

Clemens, Sydney G. A Dr. Martin Luther King, Jr. Curriculum: Playing the Dream. *Young Children, 43*(2), 6–11, 59–63. 1988.

Cole, Ann, Carolyn Haas, Elizabeth Heller, & Betty Weinberger. *Children Are Children Are Children* (illustrated by Lois Axeman). Boston, MA: Little, Brown, 1978. Out of print.
Activity ideas based on cultures of Brazil, France, Iran, Japan, Nigeria, and USSR.

Coleman, Mick. Planning for the Changing Nature of Family Life in Schools for Young Children. *Young Children, 46*(4), 15–20. 1991.

Cook, R.E., and V.B. Armbruster. *Adapting Early Childhood Curricula: Suggestions for Meeting Special Needs.* St. Louis: Mosby.
Both new and seasoned educators will benefit from this text's analysis of teaching styles and strategies, as well as its sensitive, respectful, and nurturing focus. Each chapter provides discussion topics, activites, and references.

Davidson, Dana H. Viewpoint. Child Care as a Support for Families With Special Needs. *Young Children, 45*(3), 47–48. 1990.

Deiner, Penny Low. *Resources for Teaching Young Children with Special Needs.* New York: Harcourt Brace Jovanovich, 1983.
A resource book based on the premise that all children sometimes have special needs. Focuses on areas of need and provides ideas for curriculum adaptations and then offers activities designed to help meet needs. Looks at cultural and intellectual as well as physical needs.

de la Brosse, Beatrice. (ed.). *Children With Special Needs in Family Day Care Homes: A Handbook for Family Day Care Providers.* Also, *Children With Special Needs in Family Day Care Homes: A Handbook of Approaches and Activities for Family Day Care Home Providers.* Rosemount Center, 2000 Rosemount Avenue, N.W., Washington, DC 20010. 1988.

Drawn from the experiences of day care providers, these books offer helpful information for family day care providers who care for children with special needs. Available in English and Spanish.

Delventhol, Marion. This Is My Story—This Is My Song. *Young Children*, 46(6), 16–18. 1991.

Dimidjian, Victoria J. Holidays, Holy Days, and Wholly Dazed. *Young Children*, 44(6): 70–75. 1989.

Educating Linguistically and Culturally Diverse Preschoolers. (Special Issue). *Early Childhood Research Quarterly*, 6(3). 1991.

Edwards, Carolyn Pope (with Patricia G. Ramsey). *Promoting Social and Moral Development in Young Children*. New York: Teachers College Press, 1986. Out of print.

An examination of the social cognitive growth of children ages two through six, based on a Piagetian understanding of how children construct knowledge of themselves and their world. Includes sections on sex roles and cultural categories—along with ideas for conducting thinking games with young children on these topics. Well written with anecdotes.

Ehrlich, Virginia Z. *Gifted Children: A Guide for Parents and Teachers*. New York: Trillium Press, 1989.

Written for both teachers and parents, this discussion of giftedness includes criteria for identification, special needs, educational needs, and careers.

Fauvre, Mary. Including Young Children With "New" Chronic Illnesses in an Early Childhood Education Setting. *Young Children*, 43(6), 71–77. 1988.

Fluegelman, Andrew (ed.). *The New Games Book*. New York: Doubleday & Company, 1989.

Noncompetitive games for all ages.

Froschl, Merle, Linda Colon, Ellen Rubin, and Barbara Sprung. *Including All of Us: An Early Childhood Curriculum About Disability*. Educational Equity Concepts, 114 E. 32nd Street, New York, NY 10016 (Distributed by Gryphon House, P.O. Box 275, Mt. Rainier, MD 20712), 1984.

An inclusive curriculum designed to be nonsexist and multicultural and to increase understanding of disabilities. The three curriculum units presented—Same/Different, Body Parts, and Transportation—include activities, materials suggestions, and well-conceived rationale and guidelines. Each integrates the New Friends dolls (see listing on p. 178). Excellent curriculum model with extensive resource listing.

Furman, Erna. More Protections, Fewer Directions: Some Experiences With Helping Children Prevent Sexual Abuse. *Young Children*, 42(5), 5–7. 1987.

George, Felicia. Checklist for a Non-Sexist Classroom. In Sprung, Barbara, *Non-sexist Education for Young Children: A Practical Guide*. New York: Women's Action Alliance, 1975.

Gomez, Gloria. *An Introductory Guide to Bilingual-Bicultural/Multicultural Education: Beyond Tacos, Eggrolls and Grits*. Dubuque, IA: Kendall/Hunt, 1982. Out of print.

A guide designed to help programs and individuals examine philosophies and approaches to multicultural education. Questions to promote thought and discussion and self-assessment tools.

Gonzalez-Mena, Janet. Taking a Culturally Sensitive Approach in Infant–Toddler Programs. *Young Children*, 47(2), 4–9. 1992.

Green, Marion, and Ellen Widoff. Special Needs Child Care: Training Is a Key Issue. *Young Children*, 45(3), 60–61.

Greenberg, Polly. Ideas That Work With Young Children: How to Institute Some Simple Democratic Practices Pertaining to Respect, Rights, Roots, and Responsibilities in Any Classroom (Without Losing Your Leadership Position). *Young Children*, 47(5), 10–17. 1992.

Greenberg, Polly. Ideas That Work With Young Children. Learning To Teach Native Americans? Or Learning to Teach People, Including Native Americans? *Young Children*, 47(6), 27–30, 79–81. 1992.

Haegert, Dorothy. *Children of the First People*. Tillacum Library, 202–986 Homer Street, Vancouver, BC, Canada V6B 2W7, 1983.

Beautiful photographs of Native Canadian Indians portray contemporary culture. Accompanying narratives by Native Elders recall the past. Not designed for young children—but photographs make it a valuable resource.

Hale, Janice. The Transmission of Cultural Values to Young African American Children. *Young Children*, 46(6), 7–15. 1991.

Hale-Benson, Janice E. *Black Children: Their Roots, Culture, and Learning Styles* (rev ed.). Baltimore: Johns Hopkins University Press, 1986.

Hale-Benson forcefully highlights the importance of both educators and parents understanding the bicultural process, the points of conflict between mainstream culture and African American culture, and painful obstacles that even well-meaning teachers create when they are ignorant of cultural and political context.

Harris, Violet J. Research in Review. Multicultural Curriculum: African American Children's Literature. *Young Children*, 46(2), 37–44. 1991.

Heekin, Shelley, and Patricia Mengel (eds.). *New Friends*. Chapel Hill Training-Outreach Project, 800 Eastowne Drive, Chapel Hill, NC 27514. 1983.

A preschool-kindergarten curriculum designed to help teachers provide accurate information about disabilities to young children and families of children with special needs through the use of teacher-made dolls. Teacher's Manual includes instructions for doll construction, suggestions for leading discussions on specific disabilities, ideas for related classroom activities, and guidelines for answering children's questions and exploring feelings and attitudes. Trainer's Notebook for conducting workshops on the New Friends program and an introductory slide/tape presentation are also available.

Heitz, True. How Do I Help Jacob? *Young Children*, 45(1), 11–15. 1989.

Hofschield, Kathryn A. The Gift of a Butterfly. *Young Children*, 46(3), 3–6. 1991.

Holder-Brown, Loreta, and Howard P. Parette, Jr. Children With Disabilities Who Use Assistive Technology: Ethical Considerations. *Young Children*, 47(6), 73–77. 1992.

Hrncir, Elizabeth J., and Corinne E. Eisenhart. Use With Caution: The "At–Risk" Label. *Young Children*, 46(2), 23–27. 1991.

Hungry Wolf, Adolf and Beverly. *Children of the Sun*. New York: William Morrow and Company, 1987. Out of print.

Resource for images of Indian family life as it once was.

Ihle, E.L. (Brochure). Minority Women in Teaching (Part One). Deciding to Become a Teacher. Harrisonburg, VA: James Madison University, 1991.

Jones, Elizabeth, and Louise Derman-Sparks. Meeting the Challenge of Diversity. *Young Children*, 47(2), 12–18. 1992.

Karnes, Merle B., and Lawrence J. Johnson. Training for Staff, Parents, and Volunteers working With Gifted Young Children, Especially Those With Disabilities and From Low-Income Homes. *Young Children*, 44(3), 49–56. 1989.

Kendall, Frances E. *Diversity in the Classroom*. New York: Teachers College Press, 1983.

Multicultural education comes about through a thorough understanding of child development, examination of our own attitudes, the support of parents, and careful preparation of the environment and the curriculum. Guidelines are given for developing a curriculum unit based on diversity. Extensive bibliography.

Keogh, B.K. (ed.). *Advances in Speical Education, Vol. 5. Developmental Problems in Infancy and the Preschool Years*. Greenwich, Conn.: JAI Press.

Specific topics in this volume include Developmental Perspectives on the Concept of Risk, Developmental Risk in Infants, Developmental Disabilities in Preschool Children, Language Disorders, Social and Behavioral Problems, and Problems in Motor Development. The authors effectively use discussions of theoretical models, particularly the transactional model, as a tool to illustrate areas needing further research.

Kostelnik, Marjorie J., Alice P. Whiren, and Laura C. Stein. Living With He-Man: Managing Superhero Fantasy Play. *Young Children, 41*(4), 3–9. 1986.

Kunjufu, J. *Developing Positive Self-Images and Discipline in Black Children*. Chicago: African-American Images, 1984.

Kunjufu examines the politics of educating African American children and recommends that parents and educators expose and adopt an African perspective in order to develop these children's self-esteem and discipline. Much of what is advocated is workable for all children.

Lee, Rhonda (ed.). *Guide to Nonsexist Language and Visuals*. University of Wisconsin–Extension, 432 North Lake Street, Madison, WI 53706, 1985.

A helpful guide for replacing sexist references with liberating terms.

Little Soldier, Lee. Working With Native American Children. *Young Children, 47*(6), 15–21. 1992.

McCormick, Linda, and Rita Holden. Homeless Children: A Special Challenge. *Young Children, 47*(6), 61–67. 1992.

McNeill, Earldene, Velma Schmidt, & Judy Allen. *Cultural Awareness for Young Children*. Dallas, TX: The Learning Tree (distributed by Addison-Wesley Publishing Co., Inc., Jacob Way, Reading, MA 01867), 1991.

Curriculum ideas for Asian, Black, Cowboy, Eskimo, Mexican, and Native American cultures. Excellent resource.

Meddin, Barbara J. Child Abuse and Neglect: Prevention and Reporting. *Young Children, 41*(4), 26–30. 1986.

Meltzer, Milton (ed.). *The Black Americans: A History in Their Own Words*. New York: Thomas Y. Crowell, 1964.

A resource for self-enlightenment and background information for classroom discussion and storytelling, the history of Black Americans is told through pieces of their own writings—dramatic and real.

Morrow, Robert D. What's in a Name? In Particular, a Southeast Asian Name? *Young Children, 44*(6), 20–23. 1989.

Multicultural Project for Communication and Education. *Caring for Children in a Social Context: Eliminating Racism, Sexism and Other Patterns of Discrimination*. Cambridge MA: The Multicultural Project for Communication and Education. Out of print.

A thoughtful discussion of patterns of discrimination, with specific suggestions for liberating your program or your classroom. Excellent resource for examining where you are and planning what you want to become.

National Black Child Development Institute. *African American Literature for Young Children*. (Brochure). Washington, DC: NAEYC. 1992.

This resource list of children's books includes literary works that provide accurate and realistic images of Black people and reinforce the importance of African American cultural traditions.

Orlick, Terry. *The Cooperative Sports & Games Book*, Vols. 1 & 2. New York: Pantheon Books, 1978, 1982.

Ideas for cooperative play, adaptable to a variety of ages and needs.

Paley, Vivian Gussin. *White Teacher*. Cambridge, MA: Harvard University Press, 1979.

This is a story of self-discovery told through the experiences of a White kindergarten teacher and her group of children, Black and White. She moves from being unable to talk about differences to become an adult guide, comfortably answering and asking questions, helping children to understand themselves and each other—acquiring social and intellectual skills necessary for improving life.

Peterson, N.L. *Early Intervention for Handicapped and At-Risk Children*. Denver: Love Publishing Company, 1987.

This volume provides a comprehensive overview of early childhood special education through 12 chapters grouped into three content areas: an overview, a description of the special children, and a discussion of service delivery. The reference list is comprehensive and the indexes are valuable and detailed.

Phillips, Carol Brunson. Nurturing Diversity for Today's Children and Tomorrow's Leaders. *Young Children,* 43(2), 42–47. 1988.

Pogrebin, Letty Cottin. *Growing Up Free: Raising Your Child in the 80's.* New York: McGraw-Hill, 1980.
An in-depth consideration of the impact of sex roles and sexism as they mold the lives of children. A strong statement with practical suggestions for working to help children reach their full potential.

Pueschel, S.M., J.C. Bernier, and L.E. Weidenman. *The Special Child: A Source Book for Parents of Children With Developmental Disabilities.* Baltimore: Paul H. Brookes, 1988.
The book could best be used to assist professionals in parent counseling and probably should be available to lend to parents. People who work with young children but have not been trained specifically in special education will find this book an excellent tool for understanding the needs of the children and the families with whom they work.

Quintero, Elizabeth, and M. Cristina Velarde. Intergenerational Literacy: A Developmental, Bilingual Approach. *Young Children, 45*(4), 10–15. 1990.

Ramsey, Patricia G. *Teaching and Learning in a Diverse World.* New York: Teachers College Press, 1986.
A multicultural perspective can be built into all programs and all aspects of the curriculum. Early childhood educators have a rich opportunity for creating new and liberated understanding in young children. Extensive practical suggestions.

Ramsey, Patricia G., and Louise Derman-Sparks. Viewpoint. Multicultural Education Reaffirmed. *Young Children, 47*(2), 10–11. 1992.

Rappaport, Lisa. *Recipes for Fun: Play Activities and Games for Young Children With Disabilities and Their Families* (illustrated by Ingrid Gehle). Washington, DC: Let's Play to Grow. 1986. Out of print.
This resource is filled with ideas for games and play activities that children and adults can enjoy as they explore the world together. Adaptations for specific impairments included.

Robinson, Bryan E. The Teacher's Role in Working With Children of Alcoholic Parents. *Young Children,* 45(4), 68–73. 1990.

Ross, Helen W. Integrating Infants With Disabilities? Can "Ordinary" Caregivers Do It? *Young Children,* 47(3), 65–71. 1992.

Saracho, Olivia N., and Bernard Spodek (eds.). *Understanding the Multicultural Experience in Early Childhood Education.* Washington, DC: NAEYC, 1983.
A scholarly collection of varied concerns about the impact and implications of early childhood education for different cultural groups.

Schmidt, Velma E., and Earldene McNeill. *Cultural Awareness: A Resource Bibliography.* Washington, DC: NAEYC, 1978. Out of print.
Extensive annotated bibliography of resources, listed by cultural group. Includes books for children; materials and experiential resources; and books, articles, and catalogs for adults.

Schuman, Jo Miles. *Art From Many Hands: Multicultural Art Projects.* Worcester, MA: Davis Publications, 1981.
Authentic arts and crafts from many cultures. Not targeted to young children; excellent teacher resource for inspiration and background.

Schwartz, S. (ed.). *Choices in Deafness: A Parent's Guide.* Kensington, MD: Woodbine House. 1987.
This book presents information concerning cued speech, auditory-oral communication, and total communication through succinct essays by parents of four families and one professional for each approach. Other chapters include overviews of deafness from medical, audiological, and historical perspectives.

Shannon-Thornberry, Milo. *The Alternate Celebrations Catalogue.* New York: The Pilgrim Press, 1982. Out of print.
Discussion of the messages inherent in our ways of celebrating and in our choices of things to celebrate. Suggestions for more meaningful celebrations.

Sheldon, Amy. "Kings Are Royaler Than Queens": Language and Socialization. *Young Children, 45*(2), 4–9. 1990.

Sholtys, Katherine C. A New Language, A New Life. *Young Children,* 44(3), 76–77. 1989.

Slapin, B., D. Seale, and R. Gonzalez. How to Tell the Difference: A Checklist for Evaluating Children's Books for Anti-Indian Bias. Available through New Society Publishers, 4527 Springfield Avenue, Philadelphia, PA 19143. 1991.

Smith, Jamie C. *Beginning Early: Adult Responsibilities to Gifted Young Children.* New York: Trillium Press, 1986.

A comprehensive list (in checklist format) of the responsibilities involved for administrators, teachers, parents, and programs in nurturing the growth of gifted children.

Soto, Lourdes D. Research in Review. Understanding Bilingual/Bicultural Young Children. *Young Children,* 46(2), 30–36. 1991.

Souweine, Judith, Sheila Crimmins, and Carolyn Mazel. *Mainstreaming: Ideas for Teaching Young Children.* Washington, DC: NAEYC, 1981.

Approaches and strategies for integrating children with special needs into the early childhood classroom—developing an individualized educational plan, designing the environment, and planning the curriculum.

Sprung, Barbara (ed.). *Perspectives on Non-Sexist Early Childhood Education.* New York: Teachers College Press, 1978.

A collection of thought-provoking articles related to issues of sexism in early childhood. Some pieces discuss research, while others examine theory and practice.

Texas Department of Human Resources. *Culture and Children.* Texas Department of Human Resources, Media Services Division, P.O. Box 149030 E–205, Austin, TX 78714, 1984.

Ideas for classroom activities and suggestions for resources—based on cultural groups in Texas.

van Straalen, Alice. *The Book of Holidays Around the World.* New York: E.P. Dutton, 1986.

A holiday for every day of the year (variable date explanations keep it timeless). A beautiful resource for people who like to celebrate.

Wardle, Francis. Are You Sensitive to Interracial Children's Special Identity Needs? *Young Children,* 42(2), 53–59. 1987.

Wardle, Francis. Endorsing Children's Differences: Meeting the Needs of Adopted Minority Children. *Young Children,* 45(5), 44–46. 1990.

Wardle, Francis. *Biracial Identity: An Ecological Development Model.* Denver: Center for the Study of Biracial Children. 1992.

Wenning, Jessie, and Sheli Wortis. *Made By Human Hands: A Curriculum for Teaching Young Children About Work and Working People.* Cambridge, MA: The Multicultural Project for Communication and Education, Inc. Out of print.

A well-conceived curriculum about work that reflects diversity and contemporary realities. Begins with the work of both adults and children within the center, then moves out into the family and community.

White, Barbara P., with Michael A. Phair. "It'll Be a Challenge!" Managing Emotional Stress in Teaching Disabled Children. *Young Children,* 41(2), 44–48. 1986.

Williams, Leslie R., and Yvonne De Gaetano. *Alerta.* Menlo Park, CA: Addison-Wesley Publishing Company, 1985.

An excellent guide for developing a multicultural bilingual program based on the experiences and observations of the children within the program. Content grows from the children in the context of their cultures and communities and permeates all areas of learning and activity. Valuable planning guide.

York, Stacey. *Roots & Wings: Affirming Culture in Early Childhood Programs.* St. Paul, MN: Redleaf Press, 1991.

Stacey York's book has a wonderful store of activities to use with young children, an authoritative discussion of how prejudice develops, and a sensible approach to the process of creating personal and social change.

Newsletters and organizations

The Council for Exceptional Children, 1920 Association Drive, Reston, VA 22091–1589, (703) 620–3660.

Council on Interracial Books *Bulletin,* P.O. Box 1263, New York, NY 10023. (quarterly)

Equal Play, Women's Action Alliance, 370 Lexington Avenue, New York, NY 10017, (212) 532–8330. (Twice a year)

Faces: The Magazine About People, Cobblestone Publishing, 7 School Street, Peterborough, NH 03458, (603) 924–7209. (9 issues per year)

News Digest, National Information Center for Children and Youth with Disabilities, Box 1492, Washington, DC 20013, (800) 999–5599.

Equipment, toys, and materials

NAEYC Editor's Note:

Try getting appropriate equipment, toys, and materials through your usual school supply distributor. Several of them have been pioneers in meeting teachers' needs for multicultural and individually necessary resources. We commend any and all innovators! If you find an item that is said to be appropriate, use your judgment—is the item really appropriate? If not, don't buy it! In this case, or if the dealer doesn't carry multicultural or other suitable and situation-sensitive resources, be an advocate! Explain what's needed. Then buy what you need elsewhere. Business people respond to demand. So demand! (politely, of course)

Several of the authors whose work is included in this book say that they have had increasingly good luck in finding excellent resources listed in some of the major early childhood education suppliers' catalogs, such as the following:

Community Playthings and Rifton Equipment for the Handicapped, Route 213, Rifton, NY 12471, (800) 777–4244 or (800) 374–3866.

Gryphon House, P.O. Box 275, Mt. Rainier, MD 20712, (800) 638–0928 [in Maryland, (301) 779–6200].

Kaplan School Supply Corp., P.O. Box 609, Lewisville, NC 27023, (800) 334–2014.

Lakeshore Learning Materials, P.O. Box 6261, Carson, CA 90749, (800) 421–5354.

Weston Woods, Weston, CT 06883–1199, (800) 243–5020 [in Connecticut, (203) 226–3355].

Some of the authors of this book suggest that you also try the following speciality sources:

ARTS Inc., 32 Market Street, New York, NY 10002, (212) 962–8231.
Chinese and Hispanic music, activities, and games—booklets and cassettes. Also an interesting tape of ethnic lullabies from New York City.

Claudia's Caravan, P.O. Box 1582, Alameda, CA, 94501 (415) 521–7871.
An extensive collection of multilingual, multicultural materials.

Creative Concepts For Children, P.O. Box 8697, Scottsdale, AZ 85252, (602) 483–9130.

Nonsexist, multicultural puppets. Also made to order and personalized.

Early Learning Experiences, Asper Folta Consultants, P.O. Box 729, Haines, AK 99827, (907) 766–2580.
Curriculum materials reflecting Alaskan cultures.

Educational Records, 3233 Burnt Mill Drive, Suite 100, Wilmington, NC 28403, (800) 438–1637.
Records.

The Fibar Group, 141 Halstead Avenue, Mamaroneck, NY 10543, (800) FIBAR–A1 [in New York, (914) 835–1511].
New playground surface makes play area accessible for children using wheelchairs, crutches, or walkers. Sounds good—check it out.

Hal's Pals, For Challenged Kids by Mattel, Inc., 5150 Rosecrans Avenue, Hawthorne, CA 90250, (800) 227–3800.
Dolls with physical disabilities and their own special equipment (only Black and White races available).

Harper Audio, 10 E. 53rd Street, New York, NY 10022, (800) 331–3761.
Records and cassettes.

Howe Press, Perkins School for the Blind, 175 North Beacon Street, Watertown, MA 02172, (617) 924–3434.
Writing devices for the blind.

Kar-Ben Copies, Inc., 6800 Tildenwood Lane, Rockville, MD 20852, (301) 984–8733.
Books reflecting the Jewish tradition.

Lauri puzzle, "Familiar People," available through many early childhood materials catalogs.
Represents the variety in human life. Excellent.

Music for Little People, P.O. Box 1460, Redway, CA 95560, (800) 346–4445 [in California and Alaska, (707) 923–3991].
Compact disks, cassettes, videos, games, and interesting musical instruments.

Pacific Cascade Records, 47534 McKenzie Highway, Vida, OR 97488–9707, (503) 896–3290.
Records and cassette tapes.

Pueblo to People, P.O. Box 2545, Houston, TX 77252–2545.
Handcrafted items from Central America. Note textiles.

Save the Children's Craft Shop, 54 Wilton Road, Westport, CT 06880, (203) 226–7271.
Items from around the world. Note instruments.

Smithsonian Folkways Recordings, Smithsonian Institution, 955 L'Enfant Plaza, Suite 2600, Washington, DC 20560, (202) 287–3251.
Recordings.

Keep in Shape

with

These Practical Resources for Teachers and Directors

from the creators
of **Alike and Different**

Child Care Information Exchange
The Directors' Magazine

For 15 years **Child Care Information Exchange** has been THE management magazine for directors of early childhood programs. Each bimonthly issue is packed with practical ideas a director can put to immediate use — ideas on staff motivation, raising money, parent relations, curriculum planning, staff training, leadership, building enrollment, center design, news and trends, and legal issues. **(6 issues/year, $35)**

Confronting Your Bottom Line:
Financial Guide for Child Care Centers
by Keith Stephens, CPA

An invaluable financial management guidebook for center directors and owners. Topics addressed include developing your business plan, break-even analysis, sources of funds, leasing space, plus a financial analysis of for profit child care. **(48 pages, paper, $25)**

Caring Spaces, Learning Places:
Children's Environments That Work
by Jim Greenman

Filled with practical advice on aesthetics, acoustics, room arrangement, outdoor environments, buildings and grounds, storage, and the process of change. Much more than a how-to book — a delightful collection of observations and reflections, problems and solutions, ideas and idea-sparkers, representing the best of current thinking. **(218 pages, paper, $29)**

Connecting:
Friendship in the Lives of Young Children
and Their Teachers
edited by Dennie Palmer Wolf

A look at friendship as it develops in child care centers. Insights on the nature of friendship as well as practical tools and ideas for facilitating positive relationships among children and adults. Includes chapters on infant friendships, slow to approach children, gender issues, and cultural and racial factors. A Beginnings Book for Teachers of Young Children — #10. **(128 pages, paper, $10)**

The *Anti-Ordinary* Thinkbook
by Bonnie Neugebauer

A stimulating tool for staff training and team-building in early childhood programs. Use the exercises as catalysts to innovative thinking in your program, use them as ice-breakers, as problem-solvers, as idea-sparkers. Use them to determine where you are going, how each of you perceives the program you offer, where the conflicts and difficulties lie. Let them be the beginnings of some of the most exciting, team-building staff sessions you've ever held. **(24 pages, paper, $10)**

Call in your order today — toll free
(800) 221-2864

Information About NAEYC

NAEYC is . . .

. . . a membership-supported organization of people committed to fostering the growth and development of children from birth through age eight. Membership is open to all who share a desire to serve and act on behalf of the needs and rights of young children.

NAEYC provides . . .

. . . educational services and resources to adults who work with and for children, including

• *Young Children,* the journal for early childhood educators

• **Books, posters, brochures,** and **videos** to expand your knowledge and commitment to young children, with topics including infants, curriculum, research, discipline, teacher education, and parent involvement

• An **Annual Conference** that brings people from all over the country to share their expertise and advocate on behalf of children and families

• **Week of the Young Child** celebrations sponsored by NAEYC Affiliate Groups across the nation to call public attention to the needs and rights of children and families

• **Insurance plans** for individuals and programs

• **Public affairs information** for knowledgeable advocacy efforts at all levels of government and through the media

• The **National Institute for Early Childhood Professional Development,** providing resources and services to improve professional preparation and development of early childhood educators

• The **National Academy of Early Childhood Programs,** a voluntary accreditation system for high-quality programs for children

• The **Information Service,** a centralized source of information sharing, distribution, and collaboration

For free information about membership, publications, or other NAEYC services . . .

• call NAEYC at 202–232–8777 or 800–424–2460

• or write to the National Association for the Education of Young Children, 1509 16th St., N.W., Washington, DC 20036–1426.